Staging Memories

Staging Memories

Hou Hsiao-hsien's *A City of Sadness*

Abé Mark Nornes and Emilie Yueh-yu Yeh

Maize Books: An Imprint of Michigan Publishing

Published in the United States of America by
Michigan Publishing
Manufactured in the United States of America

2018   2017   2016   2015   4   3   2   1

ISBN 978-1-60785-338-1 (paper)
ISBN 978-1-60785-339-8 (e-book)

An imprint of Michigan Publishing, Maize Books serves the publishing needs
of the University of Michigan community by making high-quality scholarship
widely available in print and online. It represents a new model for authors
seeking to share their work within and beyond the academy, offering streamlined
selection, production, and distribution processes. Maize Books is intended as a
complement to more formal modes of publication in a wide range of disciplinary
areas.

Contents

Contents

Note on Romanization of Chinese

Regarding the romanization of Chinese words and names, we have mixed systems. In order to avoid confusing the reader, we followed the English subtitles of the film for characters' names. Otherwise, we use Pinyin for the credits and bibliography. At the same time, we have not converted names and places that are well known to readers under different spellings, such as Chiang Kai-shek (Jiang Jieshi), Hou Hsiao-hsien (Hou Xiaoxian), Taipei (Taibei), Peking Opera (Beijing Opera), and the like.

Foreword to the Maize Editions

As far as we can ascertain, this was the first hypertextual analysis in film studies. It was originally the term-end project for a course in close-textual analysis at the University of Southern California in 1993. Up to that point the course had been based on the semester-long analysis of a single 35mm print. The year we took it the department brought in Michael Friend (head of the Academy of Motion Picture Arts and Sciences' archive) to teach the course. Friend was one of the first archivists plunging into the implications of digital for film preservation, so he was a perfect choice for forgoing the 35mm print and test-driving a proprietary software the USC library was developing. The USC software basically allowed for hypertextual writing (based on Mosaic, the first software for browsing the Net) and the driving of a laser-disc player. Teams in the close analysis class had to choose a film available on laser disc (LD) and write a hypertext analysis. Links in the text would call on the LD player to jump to a specific point in the film.

This was cutting-edge digital humanities in 1993. It was also extremely clunky. Because feature films did not fit on the platter-like laser discs, feature films were chopped up into four or more parts on multiple discs. When one called up a clip, the software would instruct the reader to insert the proper side of the proper disc. There was also an issue with access, considering the LD of *City of Sadness* was a nearly impossible-to-find Taiwanese pressing; we discovered it for rent in a Chinese grocery store in Monterey Park. (As of this writing, the film is available on out-of-print DVDs, but a conflict over copyright has held up the release of a Blu-ray as well as easy circulation on 35mm.)

Many of the other essays from the class were straight, linear film analyses, using hypertextual links only for calling up clips. By way of contrast, we jumped on the opportunity to tamper with the conventions of academic writing. We conjured a structure that was thoroughly dispersed and interconnected through hyperlinks. It did have an introduction and conclusion; however, the reader could freely navigate the body of the analysis. There were four main areas—we did not think of them as chapters—along with an assortment of other approaches to the film. These included a section on Hou's representation of violence, as well as a "distant analysis" that attempted to synthesize all the issues we raised in the dispersed close analyses by working, shot by shot, through a single sequence of the film—an alternative to a conclusion.

Even while the course was running, we chafed at the restrictions the software imposed upon us. It was proprietary, so anyone wanting to read the essay would have to procure the software package from USC. At that point, it did not handle still photographs very well. Most important, if one did not have access to the LD in Monterey Park—what was probably the only copy in North America—the whole system was defeated. It was a fascinating experience, but felt pointless in the end because of the virtual impossibility of disseminating the writing. However, as students we were obligated to use their closed system.

It was obvious to us that the Internet was the solution. The course was held right about the time that Mosaic browser was released, bringing the World Wide Web to those outside of the hard sciences and the military. This was a form of hypertext that put the USC software to shame. It was far more spry in terms of both markup (software tags for the display of digital texts) and calling up pages. One could link into the vast reaches of the Internet. It handled still photographs with no problem, and one could even make clickable graphics. And while it could not control a laser disc player, it did offer tantalizing possibilities for including sound and moving image. Alas, Hou's long-take aesthetic, with its delicate and complicated mise-en-scène, was completely incompatible with the rudimentary technologies for delivering movies online.

Nevertheless, immediately after the course was over, we taught ourselves html 1.0. Back then there was no support software to make this an easy task. One had to learn the code and input commands in a simple text editor. Within a matter of months, we were able to convert the close-textual analysis to an Internet-ready set of text files. A website called *Cinemaspace* caught our eye. It had just been established as one of the first online film journals by

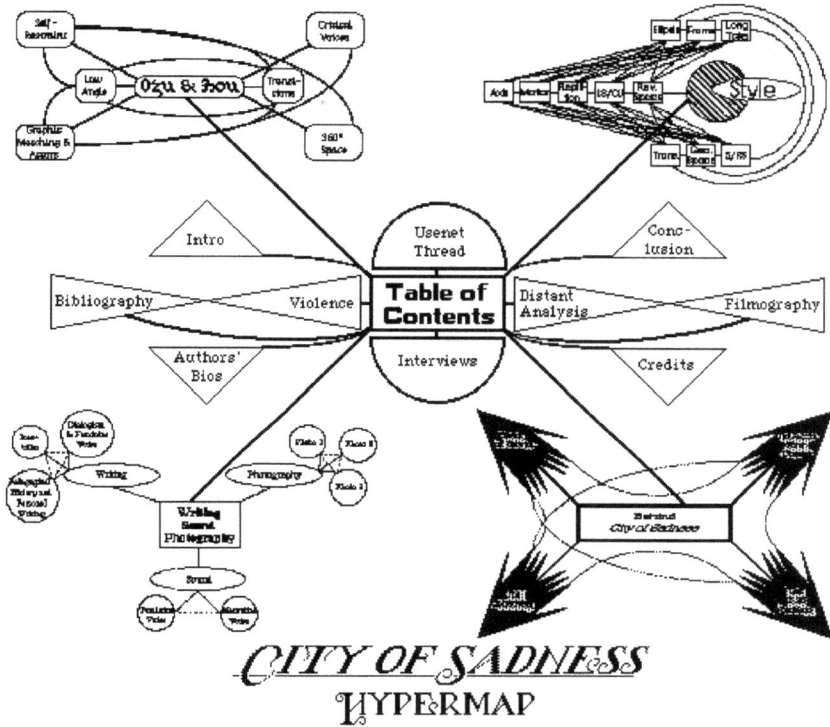

CITY OF SADNESS
HYPERMAP

This map charts the basic contours of our analysis of the film. Press on components of the map to see a more detailed view or to move to that section of the text.

Fig. 1. This was a clickable map from the original website representing the text's dispersed structure. Readers were invited to range through the text on the path of their choice. Clicking on any text on the map would send the reader to that section of the analysis.

Alex Cohen, a lecturer at Berkeley. We proposed that he publish our piece. He was delighted to have authors and content, and we were happy to have a place to host the project.

Narrating National Sadness went online in 1994, the year of the first CERN (European Organization for Nuclear Research) conference on the World Wide Web (the "Woodstock of the Web") and the year that Netscape was released. The original URL was http://cinemaspace.berkeley.edu/Pa pers/CityOfSadness/table.html. Our text had an introduction and conclusion, but everything in between could be navigated in any order. We had flat maps of the entire text's shape, and each section had its own smaller map.

Some of our sections had relatively lengthy passages, with numbered section headings that invited readers to work through a recommended order (for example, the "Sound/Writing/Photography" section); other sections were randomized snippets of analysis (e.g., the "Style" section). Our hope was that readers would explore at their own pace and be guided only by their personal inclinations.

One of the virtues of online publishing is that the final form need not be "final" in any serious sense. *Narrating National Sadness* has thus had a number of iterations that led to the present version under the Maize Books imprint. The 1994 CERN conference on the World Wide Web was also where VRML was first proposed, a virtual reality markup language analogous to html that would enable manipulable, interactive graphics online. In 1997 VRML was sufficiently developed that we dabbled in this and made a virtual reality interface for the text.

This interface had 3D graphics of extruded Chinese characters that floated in virtual space, each orbited by flat images from the film. The characters all had some semantic connection to the text they pointed to. Pointing to a radical on the character, a section title would float into view; clicking sent the reader to the text. It was essentially an interactive, 3D table of contents. It worked, but there were a couple of problems. First, the files were remarkably lean, but one still needed a very fast computer to handle them. Second, that computer had to be a PC; the 3D world didn't care for Apple. Third, and most unfortunate, we were too close to the bleeding edge for our own good, marking up the files in VRML 1.0. It wasn't long before VRML 2.0 was released, rendering anything made in the earlier version completely useless. We have reconstructed one of the graphics for the e-book for posterity's sake, but the code of original files is untranslatable gibberish.

Later, in 1997, we returned to the website and updated a few things. The Net had sufficiently developed to handle moving images and sound that was still rudimentary, but good enough to try. The movies were the size of postage stamps, and not terribly useful for Hou's film aesthetic based on long shots and long takes. But we added some clips.

For whatever reason, *Cinemaspace* never took off. Perhaps it was the typical danger of early adoption—there simply were not enough readers to produce writers for the site. Perhaps Cohen just didn't have the support or energy. He did publish a few other articles, including one on *Star Trek,* but that was about all. Still, *Narrating National Sadness* sat there online, and over the years we were regularly thanked by Chinese studies scholars and students. It was being used to teach Hou all over the world. And it has been ever since.

However, at some moment in the late 2000s, we learned that the site had mysteriously disappeared. The links around the world went dead. As for the original files, they went missing from *Cinemaspace*. To our surprise, the Wayback Machine captured only a partial archive of the site. And the backup copies we made to CD-ROMs all disappeared. Thankfully, we finally found a set of text files and about a third of the still images in the recesses of an office computer. With these files we reconstructed the analysis in a linear form for this Maize edition in paper and electronic forms. Someday in the future, perhaps a new technological platform for publishing will inspire us to return to *Staging Memories* to issue yet another edition in yet another form.

Acknowledgments

We would like to thank Michael Friend, who taught a graduate seminar at the University of Southern California in 1993 where this text was originally written. Shortly after this, we self-published the project on the World Wide Web; however, in the 2000s, the site mysteriously disappeared from the Internet. We approached a variety of university presses about publishing it in e-book form, but all but one balked at the interactive form we were determined to preserve. We are grateful to the University of Michigan Press and editor Aaron McCollough for not only picking up the project but also offering to release it on paper as well. Special thanks to the Academy of Film at Hong Kong Baptist University for granting a development fund, making the paper edition possible.

Introduction

A City of Sadness (Beiqing chengshi 悲情城市), the winner of the Golden
Lion Award at the 1989 Venice Film Festival, was made by Hou Hsiao-hsien
(侯孝賢), one of the foremost filmmakers of the New Cinema of Taiwan.
Hou, along with other young filmmakers such as Edward Yang Dechang (楊
德昌, 1947–2007), belongs to a new generation that came of age after 1949,
a period of remarkable growth and change in Taiwan. With the exception
of Hou, who worked his way through apprenticeships with veteran studio
directors, the new, young directors received formal training in the West.
They broke away from the martial arts flicks, melodramatic romances, and
historical epics haunted by memories of the mainland, all of which dominated Taiwan's film industry. Hou's films deal with the changing reality of
life in Taiwan, its generation gap, and the increasing divergence between
rural and urban cultures. What further distinguishes Hou's films is the cinematic style through which he portrays changes in Taiwanese society. His
films are strongly autobiographical, thereby presenting a platform for staging memories. These can be personal or collective, encompassing changes in
modern Taiwanese society as well as the history of Taiwanese cinema.

City of Sadness is among Hou's most ambitious works and is the first
Taiwanese film to achieve a major international prize. While all his previous
films were to some extent criticized for being too personal, *City of Sadness*
ventures into history by bringing his highly developed cinematic style to
what amounts to an epic of the birth of a nation. It is the first Taiwanese
film to broach the subject of the most traumatic experience in the nation's
history, the February 28 Incident. This was a 1947 massacre by the National-

ist Party that resulted in 18,000 to 28,000 deaths. Using a family as a matrix through which to filter the historical events at the moment of the founding of the nation, Hou re-presents Taiwanese history in both micro and macro perspectives.

The film's plot is exceedingly complex, centering on the Lin family in Taiwan after the 1945 surrender of the Japanese. The family relations are so elaborate that several magazines have even published family trees to accompany articles on the film. Taiwan had been a Japanese colony for the previous fifty years until the Chinese Nationalist government began taking over the island after World War II. The oldest of four brothers in the Lin family turns his Japanese-style bar into "Little Shanghai" to cash in on the postwar boom. The second Lin brother had disappeared during the war in the Philippines. The third brother, having returned from Shanghai and recovered from a mental breakdown, associates with Shanghainese drug smugglers. However, when the first brother finds out about this drug business, he confiscates a certain amount of drugs and forbids the third brother to continue his involvement with the mainlanders. This leads the Shanghainese to use their military connections to frame the third brother, who is accused as a Japanese collaborator during the war and jailed. After the big brother reconciles with the gangsters from Shanghai, the third brother is eventually released, emerging from prison as a physical and mental wreck. The youngest brother, Lin Wen-ching, is deaf and cannot speak, and supports himself with a photo studio. Wen-ching and his circle of young friends are convinced that socialism will be the ultimate tool for the Taiwanese to repel outside colonial forces. It is a position that makes them targets of the new regime.

The violence of the February 28 Incident and the subsequent social climate transform the family. Wen-ching is arrested, along with many of his friends. Upon his release, his best friend Hinoe, having been involved in the antigovernment movement, is forced to flee to the mountains to join the guerrillas. Wen-ching also wants to join the guerrillas, but he is persuaded to stay behind and take care of Hinoe's sister, Hinomi.

Later, the older brother dies in a fight with rival gangs. Shortly after the older brother's funeral, Wen-ching marries Hinomi and they have a son. Then her brother's guerrilla encampment is raided by the military and Wen-ching is arrested. The film ends with what is left of the deeply scarred Lin family, living despite their wounds by struggling to maintain the mundane basis of their lives.

1 / Contexts

Straddling the historical, political, and cultural frontiers between the Japanese occupation and the nationalist incursion, *City of Sadness* proves a particularly dense, even baffling, film. One can hardly begin to appreciate its complexity without understanding the circumstances of the Taiwanese film industry, the historical situation of Taiwan, and the multiple rewritings of that history.

The History of Taiwan

Taiwan, originally named Tapanga by the aborigines, is an island initially inhabited by nine ethnic groups of aborigines belonging to Malayo-Polynesian system. The island was later renamed Formosa by the Portuguese. Since the 6th century, Chinese have settled on the island. Because the Chinese government originally prohibited official settlement of the island, Chinese émigrés were either fugitives or poverty-stricken peasants from the south-coast provinces.

   With the coming of European imperialism to the Pacific, settlement of the island by both the Dutch and Spanish began in 1624, and the island entered its first period of colonial occupation. Han immigrants from mainland China played the role of mediators between the colonials and the aborigines. Like many other colonized countries in Asia and Africa, the Western imperialists were interested only in colonial exploitation of the island's resources. While Taiwan became a supplier of raw materials for the Dutch, the development of the island had to wait until 1661 when Taiwan fell under the control of the Chinese. During this period, the population of Chinese immigrants rose to nearly three million. At this time, Taiwan shifted from an "immigrant society" to a "native society" (the terms are from anthropologist Chen Qinan). Painstaking assimilation or integration among various clans and subethnic groups gradually occurred. Also, the Chinese government changed its prohibition policy and encouraged emigration to Taiwan. The aborigines during this period were either "assimilated" into the dominant Han culture or forced into the interior.

In 1895, about the time of the birth of cinema, China ceded Taiwan to Japan at the end of the First Sino-Japanese War. At the advent of the 20th century, Taiwan entered another colonial period, gradually becoming what the Japanese Empire saw as a showcase of colonial modernity. During this time, infrastructure was built on the island, driven by colonial desires. The colonial government stepped up its rule in the early 1940s by forcing the Taiwanese to adopt Japanese names and speak only the Japanese language. To this day, many older people in Taiwan can speak Japanese and this is one of the many languages heard in *City of Sadness*. With Japan's defeat and surrender Taiwan was passed on to the Nationalist government on the mainland. The Taiwanese celebrated their liberation from Japan, but it soon became clear that the Chinese authorities only intended to maintain the colonial structures of exploitation. When the Taiwanese rebelled in 1947, they were met with machine guns and mass arrests, known as the February 28 Incident.

In subsequent years, Taiwan went through a series of economic and land reforms, gradually building a strong economy in spite of an authoritarian government. After Chiang Kai-shek and his son, Chiang Ching-kuo (蔣經國), died, political and social reforms rapidly unfolded. In 1987 the martial law imposed by the Nationalists since 1947 was revoked, making it possible for writers and filmmakers to broach the subject of the February 28 Incident.

The February 28 Incident

World War II came to its bloody conclusion in 1945. Japan was reeling from its fifteen years of violent war as well as the atomic atrocities in Hiroshima and Nagasaki. In the Allies' earlier meeting in Cairo, the United States, Britain, and the Soviet Union officially agreed that Taiwan's governing power should be resumed by China upon Japan's surrender. On the 25th of December in 1945, the native-born Taiwanese cheerfully celebrated their reunion with mainland China, a scene literalized early in the film. Undoubtedly, they were anticipating the freedom and democracy that would be brought to the island along with the landing of the Nationalist government.

In the course of fifty years of colonial rule by the Japanese and several decades of separation from China, Taiwan's social, legal, and cultural system had evolved into something different than that of China in the 1940s. The most disparate conflict was in language. The official language in Taiwan had been Japanese during the colonial period, and most Taiwanese under fifty years of age could neither speak nor understand Mandarin, despite the fact that the provincial dialect, Taiwanese Amoy, shares the same writing style. Lacking a means of verbal communication—as well as a mutual understanding of cultural and social specificity—a deep-seated bigotry developed between the Taiwanese civilians and the new Nationalist government. The ensuing confusion and complexity is represented in a notable scene from *City of Sadness* where a conversation between two characters necessitates translations between four languages.

Instead of resolving the tension, the Nationalist government exacerbated it through its authoritarian rule, depriving native Taiwanese of the right to share political power. Within two years after Taiwan's return to China, Taiwanese had a taste of the Kuomintang (KMT) corruption that precipitated economic depletion. The spark for the massacre came when officials from the government tobacco monopoly, backed by about a dozen police, confiscated the goods of a woman selling smuggled cigarettes. The woman was mercilessly beaten by a policeman when she resisted their actions. Their brutality outraged bystanders, sparking clashes in which a man was killed. The next day—February 28, 1947—an incensed crowd gathered in the streets of Taipei, and subsequent rebellions erupted in many parts of the island. Martial law was declared, and troops fired on the crowds. The rebellion was ultimately suppressed, but the army followed up in subsequent days and months by arresting and executing those thought to be involved. Many of those killed were the island's elites. This mass erasure of Taiwan's political and intellectual leaders and their associates became known as the February 28 Incident, or 2.28 Incident, in Taiwanese history.

With the lengthy Executive Yuan task force report on the February 28 Incident, which was released on its 45th anniversary in 1992, the KMT government admitted that its army killed an estimated 18,000 to 28,000 Taiwanese in the 1947 massacre. The report also amounts to an apology for government handling of the uprising and the subsequent four decades of Nationalist rule in Taiwan. Along with the release of the report, the taboo imposed upon the matter for four decades became a symbol for native-born Taiwanese of political struggle against the authoritarian government.

Taiwan Cinema

From the Birth of Cinema to the New Cinema

Cinema arrived on the island of Taiwan in 1901. For the first twenty years, only the Japanese made documentaries and feature films. In order to keep the colonial structure intact, the Japanese excluded any Taiwanese actors until 1922 in a film called *The Eyes of Buddha* (Fotuo zhi tong 佛陀之瞳). The first film produced locally came in 1925 with *Whose Fault Is It?* (Shei zhi guo? 誰之過?). Gradually, a vertically integrated industry formed using Taiwanese talent and capital. This was, of course, tightly controlled by the Japanese, and the local films drew on Japanese conventions in the silent era. For example, the *benshi,* the narrator who sat next to the screen and supplemented the music and images in Japan, was adopted and retermed as *bianshi* (辯士) by the Taiwanese. They also used another Japanese convention called the *rengasi* (*rensageki* in Japanese), which was a curious hybrid of film and theater that used cinema to stage spectacles for the stage. The industry was interrupted in 1937 by the Sino-Japanese War, and virtually nothing was produced until after the Nationalist government took over the island in 1945.

With the end of civil war in 1949, Shanghai filmmakers sympathetic to the Nationalists accompanied Chiang Kai-shek to Taiwan, and after the economy stabilized these exiled filmmakers formed the heart of a new film community in Taiwan in the 1950s. Like other industries on the island, the film industry slowly developed in this period with the help of government subsidy. Mandarin and low-budget dialect films constituted the core of the nation's film production. A bilingual film system only lasted for a short period. Dialect film production in Taiwanese soon declined for two reasons: (1) the government's implementation of a new language policy that excluded local dialects in the public discourse, and (2) the low-budget fare of dialect films were outclassed by the government-subsidized Mandarin films.

By the 1960s, modernization rapidly expanded on the island. Economic development, civil education, and industrialization were held as the major projects by the authorities. In 1963, the government's Central Motion Picture Corporation (CMPC) introduced "healthy realist" pictures. These optimistic films, such as *The Oyster Girl* (Ke nü 蚵女, 1964) and *Beautiful*

Ducklings (Yang ya ren jia 養鴨人家, 1965), upheld a new moral economy promoted by the party-state in contemporary society. Meanwhile, Taiwanese screens were still dominated by more popular genres such as martial arts and period pictures from Hong Kong. In addition, there were also romantic melodramas, usually based on the stories of a woman author named Qiong Yao (瓊瑤). The Qiong Yao romantic melodrama achieved huge popularity in the early 1970s, pushing the healthy realist pictures off the screen. The anxiety of reconciling modernity and tradition vis-à-vis rapid socioeconomic change was present in these melodramas, manifested through the conflict between the individual and society.

Toward the end of the 1970s, another popular genre called "social realism" emerged. Films like *The Queen Bee* (Nüwang feng 女王蜂, 1981) and *Revenge of Women* (Nüxing de fuchou 女性的復仇, 1981) featured sex, violence, and gang subcultures. The display of explicit violence and misogyny appeared to respond to government censorship of sexuality onscreen. This low-budget fare soon declined after the recycling of similar stories and banal spectacles of sex and violence.

The Emergence of the New Cinema

Beginning in the late 1970s, the local film industry was confronted with a set of challenges. Though Taiwanese society had been through tremendous changes in the previous decade, local cinema did not show an interest in making movies that were sufficiently topical. The audience gradually became tired of the standard commercial fare and its repetitive clichés. A related challenge to the film industry came from the popularity of home videos. Because the copyright law had only recently gone into effect, inexpensive, bootleg videos were a cheap form of entertainment; many households could easily rent or purchase videotapes of movies and television programs from the United States, Japan, and Hong Kong. The final challenge to Taiwanese film was the new cinema from Hong Kong. The Hong Kong New Wave had renewed Hong Kong cinema with generic innovations and star power. In the early 1980s, Hong Kong movies engulfed local films and became the mainstay of the film market.

These financial pressures forced the industry to seek new ways of competing with Hong Kong films. The first initiatives were taken by CMPC with the support of fresh, young directors. Under the supervision of the CMPC, a portmanteau film called *In Our Time* (Guangyin de gushi 光陰的故事),

composed of four distinct episodes by four new directors, was produced in 1982. It represented the first break with the old mode of filmmaking. The film is a review of social change in Taiwan over three decades. Unlike standard Taiwanese fare, this film cast non- or semiprofessional actors instead of famous stars and did not follow a traditional narrative structure or fit into any generic category. Because of these innovations, *In Our Time* is considered as a prelude to the New Cinema movement.

Yet the New Cinema did not materialize until other innovative films appeared and achieved broader recognition. In 1983, *Growing Up* (Xiaobi de gushi 小畢的故事), directed by Chen Kunhou (陳坤厚) and produced by Hou Hsiao-hsien, and another portmanteau film entitled *The Sandwich Man* (Erzi de da wan'ou 兒子的大玩偶, directed by three young filmmakers, including Hou) attracted a great deal of attention. Composed of three distinct episodes, *The Sandwich Man* can be regarded as the hallmark of the movement. The film portrays Taiwan during the Cold War period when the country developed its economy with the assistance of aid from the United States.

Despite the unifying focus on the workers, their misery, and their lack of social capital, each episode is different in style. *The Sandwich Man* attracted considerable attention in the local press, which viewed it as a break from mainstream cinema. With the commercial success and critical acclaim of *Growing Up* and *The Sandwich Man,* these new directors were granted opportunities to make more films.

Auteurs

From 1983 through 1989, approximately ten filmmakers participated in this movement, each developing his (they are exclusively male) own particular style and making his own contribution to the New Cinema. For example, Hou Hsiao-hsien's strongly autobiographical films—*The Boys from Fengkuei* (Fenggui lai de ren 風櫃來的人, 1983); *A Time to Live and a Time to Die* (Tongnian wangshi 童年往事, 1985); "Son's Big Doll," the first episode in *The Sandwich Man* (1983); *A Summer at Grandpa's* (Dongdong de jiaqi 冬冬的假期, 1984); and *Dust in the Wind* (Lian lian fengchen 戀戀風塵, 1986)—reveal a realism that is startling in its authentic and artistic portrayal of rural life in Taiwan. Because of his unique observational, documentary-like style—the use of deep focus and long takes, nonlinear narrative, ellipti-

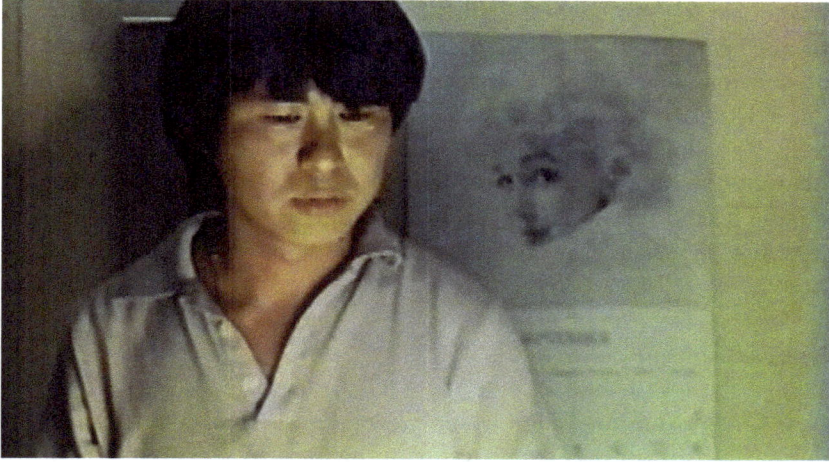

Fig. 2. Hou Hsiao-hsien starred in Edward Yang's *Taipei Story.*

cal editing, and portrayal of the daily lives of the Taiwanese—Hou Hsiao-hsien has been acclaimed as the leading auteur of Taiwan cinema by local film critics. His personal victories on the international film festival circuit, including his receipt of the Golden Lion at Venice for *City of Sadness,* represented a triumph and vindication of the Taiwanese New Cinema.

Another leading auteur of the New Cinema is Edward Yang. Regarded as Hou's cinematic equal, Yang was remarkably different from Hou in terms of style and subject matter. Unlike Hou, who always focuses on males, childhood, adolescence, and rural life, Yang was concerned with women, the newly emerging middle class, and urban society. Yang made seven feature films: *That Day, on the Beach* (Haitan de yitian 海灘的一天, 1983), *Taipei Story* (Qingmei zhuma 青梅竹馬, 1985, which starred Hou), *The Terrorizer* (Kongbu fenzi 恐怖分子, 1986), *A Brighter Summer Day* (Gulingjie shaonian sharen shijian 牯嶺街少年殺人事件, 1991), *A Confucian Confusion* (Duli shidai 獨立時代, 1994), *Mahjong* (Majiang 麻將, 1996), and *Yi Yi* (Yiyi 一一, 2000). In these works, Yang consistently addressed the social and personal problems that confront the urban, intellectual, and cultural elite in the increasingly industrialized, Japanese-influenced, and Westernized Taipei.

Because of Yang's urban emphasis, the cinematic language he employed was similar to the modernist aesthetic associated with European art cinema. In discussing his work, critics often invoked Michelangelo Antonioni, an observation Yang detested. Detached camera movement, long takes, non-linear narrative, multiple diegeses, location shots, and paratactic editing, were the hallmarks of Yang's techniques. His skillful utilization of modernist tropes, sharp observations on Taiwan's high-tech, capitalistic, alienated urban life, and retrospective look at the island's tremendous social changes were also important elements in his films.

Form and Substance

New Cinema directors, all of whom grew up in the post–World War II era during Taiwan's socioeconomic restructuring from an agricultural society to an industrialized and capitalist society, examined the various problems that the Taiwanese people had to cope with in an increasingly modernized society. In order to create a cinema that entailed a more realistic relationship with history and memory, most new films were shot on location. Under a similar notion, minor or nonprofessional actors were cast to evoke a more "true-to-life" atmosphere.

Clearly influenced by Italian neorealism, the new directors were committed to a quasi-documentary style in their filmmaking. They drew deeply on their life experiences to construct their narratives and in their deployment of mise-en-scène. Their narratives often pitted the working or peasant classes against a background of deprivation and misery. Almost every new film tried to reconstruct history to some extent. The look at the rural, agricultural past was nostalgic; the view toward the urban, industrial present was bitter. As a result, a set of thematic binary pairs can often be found in these films: rural (backward, peaceful) vs. urban (advanced, turbulent); peasant/working class (innocent, benevolent) vs. middle class (sophisticated, manipulative); past (good) vs. present (bad).

In addition to these themes, an unprecedented concern with the daily lives of local people has been shown by the new directors, particularly with respect to native cultures and languages. Because of the power struggle between the Chinese Communists and Nationalists over the four decades since World War II, the Nationalist Party insisted that the government in Taiwan represented the true China and, therefore, the real Chinese culture. Moreover, when the Nationalist army first came to Taiwan in 1945, a bloody conflict arose between the Taiwanese and the mainlanders, climaxing with the February 28 Incident. As a result, the government privileged the so-called Middle Kingdom, a culture developed by the Yellow River Valley inhabitants in China after 2000 BC, as the single culture that everyone in Taiwan must accept as their own; thus the native languages (Taiwanese Amoy, the major Fujian dialect spoken in Taiwan, and Hakka) and cultures were officially suppressed.

The New Cinema directors responded to a rise in public consciousness to return to the native and regional cultures. They used actors who speak the Taiwanese Amoy dialect to portray real-life ordinary people. Hou Hsiao-hsien may be the filmmaker who has dealt most carefully with the trilingual phenomenon (Mandarin, Taiwanese Amoy, and Hakka) in Taiwan. His *Summer at Grandpa's, A Time to Live and a Time to Die,* and *City of Sadness* present multiple dialects to oppose the government's forced monolingualism.

Another thematic reorientation by the Taiwan New Cinema was the direct reference to political and social taboos. Behind this phenomenon we may find the lifting of martial law in 1987 and the political, social, and diplomatic reform policies that followed, as well as growing demands for more radical reforms from civilian movements. Three films made in 1989—*City of Sadness, Banana Paradise* (Xiang jiao tian tang 香蕉天堂), and *Gang of Three Forever* (Tongdang wansui 童黨萬歲)—touched on political controversies that were considered highly sensitive and forbidden in public discourse before 1987.

In addition to the realist approach to subject matter, the New Cinema stands out for an additional reason: its continuing effort to explore the medium's specificity. Rather than conform to the myth that filmmaking should follow generic conventions to fulfill audience expectations, the new directors negotiated commercialism and art. They attempted to make films that sometimes agitated the audience, sometimes promoted thoughtful reflection.

Clearly influenced by Western modernist movements, the narrative structure in these films is more fragmented than linear, the editing is more obtrusive than continuous, and sentimental expression has been suspended to block emotional identification. Offscreen sound has been used frequently to convey a sense of alienation (especially in the films of Hou and Yang); the frequent use of close-ups is replaced by long takes and long shots that make for a more distanced perspective. This is particularly clear in the manner in which scenes of action are constructed, as we argue below in our analysis of the representation of violence.

However, differences exist among individual directors, even though most of them share a common purpose—exploring the full potential of filmmaking. Wan Ren, for example, despite his quite modernist approach, still emphasizes melodrama in his films. His first work, the episode in *The Sandwich Man* called "The Taste of Apples" (Pingguo de ziwei 蘋果的滋味), successfully conveys the bitter taste of the postcolonial mentality, not because of detached camerawork and fragmented narrative, but because of his use of conventional ways of creating dramatic ironies and comic effects. Another filmmaker, Zhang Yi, concentrates on depicting female psychology in a classical realist tradition. *Jade Love* (Yuqing sao 玉卿嫂, 1984) is one good example that shows his use of a classical realist narrative to articulate his criticism of feudal patriarchy.

Rejecting the stereotypical concept of filmmaking dearly held by the veteran directors as commodity and as political propaganda, the New Cinema strives for medium specificity in documenting the social and cultural realities of Taiwan. Yet this bourgeois-humanistic ideology in redirecting the look of Taiwanese cinema did generate debates when a new critical regime came into power with the rise and success of the new films. The critical regime of critics trained in Western academic contexts contested the interpretive authority of veteran critics and their institutional territory, the newspaper column. Their attention to and support of the new filmmakers involved less of an ideological struggle (i.e., Westernized aesthetic taste) than a larger question of survival and of power over the discourse. As a result, it is not surprising to see that the attack on the new films came from the veteran critics. Based on the domestic commercial disasters of the most celebrated filmmakers, such as Hou Hsiao-hsien and Edward Yang, who were criticized for their idiosyncratic and elitist taste, critics dismissed them as hardly relevant to the majority of working-class consumers.

Although the veteran critics' remarks can be easily dismissed for being simplistic and insensitive to artistic expression, it is exactly their take on the distinction between high art and low culture that provoked an interesting reconsideration of the New Cinema. As Taiwan approached the 21st century, the New Cinema almost became an obsolete term in discussing film in Taiwan. Given the fact that the New Cinema did not renovate the industry nor build up a solid reservoir of domestic films to compete with commercial product, domestic filmmaking remained vulnerable. Taiwan's film market continues to be dominated by Hollywood entertainment films. Many filmmakers who participated in the New Cinema have either ceased making films altogether or were recruited into television production. Hou Hsiao-hsien and Edward Yang, on the other hand, became the most internationally celebrated Taiwanese filmmakers, as evidenced by Hou's coups at the Venice Film Festival for *City of Sadness* and *The Puppetmaster* (Xi meng rensheng 戲夢人生, 1993).

The question of how and why New Cinema was eventually rejected by the audience requires further investigation. The more productive and fruitful approach to examine this question will rely upon reconceptualizing our understanding of national cinema in Taiwan. The question of art cinema and popular cinema in relation to the industrial and commodity system in Taiwan seems to be the main issue underlying the many objections raised against the new directors, a consideration that has been ignored for too long and too easily. These are, of course, questions beyond the scope of the present project. By raising these issues, however, we hope to at least provide a provocative backdrop for our analysis of *City of Sadness*.

The *City of Sadness* Controversy

The rapid political and social restructuring of the late 1980s and the rescinding of martial law in 1987 gave the public an opportunity to pressure the government to disclose the files of the February 28 Incident. The dialogism surrounding the rewriting of the February 28 Incident has become a major discursive battlefield in many political debates. In 1992, in response to increasing demands, an official report was published in which the government admitted that its army killed an estimated 18,000 to 28,000 native-born Taiwanese in the 1947 massacre. This document not only acknowledged that corruption and misrule were fundamental causes for the riot but also overwrites the original official report published in 1947, *The 2.28 Incident Investigation Report,* which insists that the riot was instigated by the Chinese Communist Party and therefore justified the violent suppression as an unavoidable chapter in the continuing struggle against Communism.

However, political scholars and historians from the opposition have indicated that despite its figures, the 400,000-word 1992 document is still written in the logic of historical determinism that refuses to acknowledge that the contradictions and strong arm of colonialism should be held responsible for the "unavoidable" conflict.

In addition to the government's report in 1992, other efforts at recollecting the memory and history of the incident have emerged. For example, a 686-page collection of eyewitness accounts and supporting documents was compiled by the Taiwan Provincial Historical Commission in November 1991. The multiple discourses competing for the legitimate authorship of documenting the February 28 Incident seem to imply the problematic of a total history and, consequently, the concomitant problematic of a total filmic representation of the February 28 Incident.

Death of the New Cinema

Death of the New Cinema, a book published in Chinese in 1991, provides an example of a counteranalysis of *City of Sadness* influenced by the exigencies of political debates. Given the success of *City of Sadness* and Hou's status as the most renowned filmmaker in Taiwan, *Death of the New Cinema* was written by a marginalized group of film critics as an alternative voice to the unified critical discourse surrounding *City of Sadness.* They argued against *City of Sadness* for its ambiguous representation of Taiwan's history from 1945 to 1949, and its depiction of the February 28 Incident in particular. The book argues that, rather than directly confronting the brutality of the Nationalist regime, the film displaces politics with individual romance, family saga, and a life-death cycle that seem to contribute to universal values rather than provoke political consciousness.

Considering the specific historical, political, and critical contexts that mobilized farmers, workers, students, and intellectuals to engage with social movements on issues of ecology, labor unions, education, and politics in the late 1980s, it is not surprising to see a polemical counteranalysis like this emerging in film criticism. Although several articles in the book totally misread the film and end up stalled in a vulgar ideological cul-de-sac, the book's overall attempt to destabilize the "legitimate" discourse of the New Cinema must be considered as an important register in formulating dialectical analysis about the new cinema itself, and the political and social reform in Taiwan at large.

Hou's distinct style and narrative structure in *City of Sadness* are not significant merely for their breathtaking aesthetic qualities. Imbricated in this style are discursive elements such as photography, sound, writing, and female voice-over that privilege the formation of a dialogue responding to the polysemy of this historical period's recent reconstruction. The political context in late 1940s Taiwan leaves no space for militant resistance; the crackdown on Hinoe's encampment in the narrative can be taken as a diegetic representation of historical fact. However, it is the nature of this representation of history, which its multiple levels of textuality—from mise-en-scène to sound to intertitles—that make *City of Sadness* an exceedingly complicated narration of the Taiwanese nation. Rather than directly competing with the pedagogical narration of the Nationalist regime in resisting their political hegemony, these discursive textualities formulate a double writing, as well as a challenge to the grand narrative of history.

2 / A Style of Unreasonable Choices

While the world of art cinema is filled with stylists, there are only a handful of filmmakers who have developed a personal approach so idiosyncratic that it is recognizable at a glance. Hou is one of those filmmakers. And *City of Sadness* is the film that crystallized his approach to cinematic narration. It provided a foundation from which he continues to elaborate in his subsequent films.

One of the reasons Hou Hsiao-hsien has come to the attention of critics is this cinematic style which, in its systematic rigor, has few precedents in the history of cinema. At this book's initial writing, shortly after the release of *City of Sadness,* no one had brought his approach under close analysis. While it is reckless to make such assertions, we will argue that Hou's style may be considered unique in the history of cinema. In this section we hope to describe this approach with great specificity, for it is difficult to understand the power of his films without first grasping the nature of his cinema and its relationship to thematic concerns.

Hou put this approach to cinematic narration in place early in his career, and he changes in significant ways after 1995 (see James Udden, "This Time He Moves!"). However, Hou's cinema reaches a particular level of refinement in *City of Sadness,* particularly for the way cinematic style becomes inseparable from his representation of history.

Hou's style displays characteristics we may describe as self-restricting. This general orientation toward restraint and stylization is reminiscent of Ozu Yasujiro, so much so that one is tempted to borrow David Bordwell's characterization of Ozu's work as an "unreasonable style," a comparison we deal with below. In Hou's case, the following self-restrictions have been imposed to some degree on all his films:

- The use of relatively static, extremely long takes
- Measured, rhythmic use of ellipsis
- Minimal use of tracks, pans, intrashot reframing
- Temporally unmarked transitional spaces
- Tendency toward tableaux-like long shots/few closeups
- The geometricization of space
- Delimitation of the frame
- Locking the camera/spectator onto a single axis
- Rare, strategic use of the shot–reverse shot figure
- Gradual revelation and construction of spatial relationships
- Repetition

This sounds overly programmatic (a danger in any taxonomy). However, it should be emphasized that these characteristics are entirely interrelated, as the following elaboration will show. Moreover, Hou orchestrates these qualities in such a rigorous way that they lend themselves to an equally rigorous analysis. These are legible characteristics and not dogmatic rules. At the same time, we hope to show that the rare occurrences of the staples of classical filmmaking (such as the shot-reverse shot) are crucially connected to larger issues of style, theme, and cultural codes.

The Long Take (and Neorealism)

The only characteristic of Hou's style that critics consistently single out is the long take. *City of Sadness* consists of 222 shots (including intertitles). With a running time of 158 minutes, that puts the average shot length at around forty-three seconds, with individual shots reaching over three minutes long. Table 1 parses the average shot lengths in the film.

When the long take is invoked to describe a given film, closer analysis will often show that it is used only sporadically. For example, according to Barry Salt's calculations in "Statistical Style Analysis of Motion Pictures," the average shot length in Renoir's *Le Crime de M. Lange* is twenty-one seconds, for *Citizen Kane,* twelve seconds (697). In Hou's case, the long take is surprisingly consistent from the first shot to the last. Furthermore, all of his films are similarly consistent; for example, the average shot length of *Dust in*

TABLE 1. *CITY OF SADNESS*'S AVERAGE SHOT LENGTH (ASL)

NAME	LANDSCAPE	EXT. ELS	VLS	LS-MLS	MS	MCU	VARIABLE	OTHER
Number of Shots	9	16	34	42	48	19	31	24
Length:	3.41	7.09	28.57	36.03	34.06	7.95	33.27	7.31
Average Shot Length:	22.7	26.6	50.4	51.5	42.6	25.1	64.4	18.3
MSL:	21.2	22.2	43	42.2	38.6	22.8	50	13.4
MSL/ASL:	0.93	0.83	0.85	0.82	0.91	0.91	0.78	0.73
StDev:	9.6	13.6	28.5	40.6	29.8	14.4	39.3	18
Min:	12.4	11.2	8.8	8	4.8	5.2	8.4	6
Max:	38	62	117.2	201.6	134	63.3	186.8	98
CV:	0.42	0.51	0.56	0.79	0.7	0.57	0.61	0.99

Summary: ASL: 42.4, MSL: 33.6; MSL/ASL: 0.79; LEN: 157.41.6; NoS: 223; MAX: 201.6; MIN: 4.8; Range: 196.8; StDev: 33.5; CV: 0.79.

Note: Drawing on a Cinemetrics analysis of the film conducted by edo (the author's log-in name), this table describes the average shot length (ASL) in *City of Sadness*, arranged by shot size. The film has an ASL of 42.4 seconds, with lengths between 4.8 and 201.6 seconds for its 223 shots. Most of Hou's shorter shots are extreme long shots or medium close-ups. By way of contrast, the Cinemetrics analysis of *The Bourne Ultimatum* (2007), with a running time nearly an hour shorter, showed it clocking in at an ASL of 2.1 seconds over 2,871 shots.

GRAPH 1.

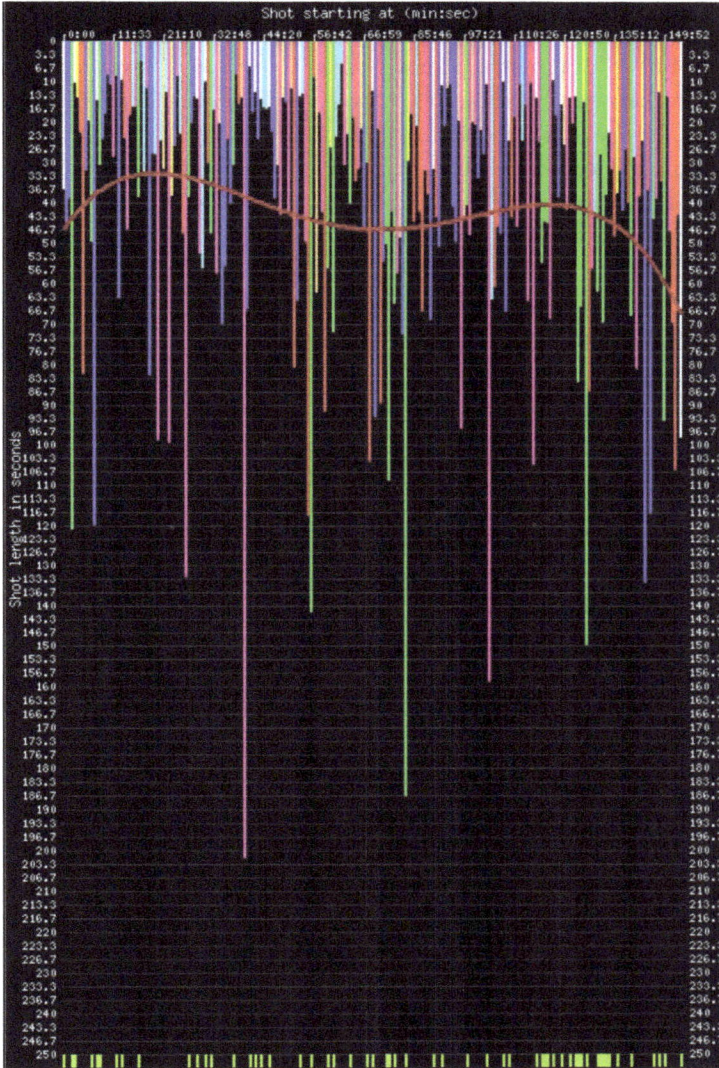

Note: This graph from Cinemetrics (created by edo) charts the length of every shot in *City of Sadness,* with the curved red line representing trends in shot length over the course of the film. The horizontal x-axis tracks the time code for the film, starting from left to right. The vertical y-axis corresponds to shot length. The colors are coded by scale (landscape to medium close-up). Thus, the longest shot in the film is a LS-MLS (long shot–medium long shot) occurring at 38:38, and it is 201.6 seconds long. The graph can be manipulated in a wide variety of ways by clicking through to the Cinemetrics website (http://www. cinemetrics.lv/movie.php?movie_ID=3282).

the Wind is thirty-four seconds. Hou said, "I renounced fragmentary editing in favor of a sweeping style of montage, cutting not for the flow of the
rhythm, but to capture the atmosphere and 'feel' of the shot and smooth
transitions between the shots" (Jay Scott, "A Cause for Rejoicing in a *City
of Sadness*"). This is not to say that there is no sense of rhythm; indeed, the
distinction in Hou's use of the long take is the expansive sense of a steady
progression of shots at the slowest of beats, articulated by a profound appli-
cation of ellipsis that is described below.

While this proclivity toward the long take nearly always invokes comparisons to Italian neorealism, there are significant differences that set Hou's
approach apart. In general, this comparison has surfaced more in regards
to New Cinema (especially for its deployment of nonactors), as neorealism
remains the standard against which any self-proclaimed realism is measured.
We suggest that Hou's narrations and most of the early New Cinema, films
such as *Kuei-mei, a Woman* (Wo zheyang guo le yisheng 我這樣過了一
生, 1985), *Ah Fei* (You ma cai zi 油麻菜籽, aka *Rapeseed Girl* 1984), and
That Day, on the Beach (1983), are essentially based on melodrama. However,
Taiwanese film tends to be more subdued than neorealism, which has moments of hysteria; it is tempting to call them "melodramas without excess."
In Hou's case, however, we will see how truly excessive his own style is. In
terms of the long take, Hou uses it in a more constant, rigorous manner than
any of the international directors it is generally identified with, especially the
neorealists.

Furthermore, while neorealism was about "Italy Now," much of the New
Cinema—particularly Hou's work—has been a search for identity through
reminiscences of "Taiwan Then." In Asian film, this brand of soul-searching
often leads to the countryside to find a more "authentic" or "pure" rem-
nant of one's culture in the face of encroaching industrialization and the
explosion of consumer culture in the city. Taiwan is a small island, though,
and modern transportation and media have shrunk the distance between
country and city, erasing the differences between the two. This positions
identity crises in the past as a site for self-examination, often using regional
literature (or those writers' scripts) as a vehicle of exploration. *City of Sadness*
works in this mode, setting the plot at the repressed site where "Taiwanese"
identity (as opposed to "Chinese") was negotiated, formed in opposition to
the arrogated centrality of the KMT. Before this moment in history, the Taiwanese relationship to the mainland was more or less unproblematic. From
the 1950s to the present, the turbulent, originary period of 1945 to 1949 remained banished from the public discourse until Hou made *City of Sadness*.

Thus neorealism is not an operative model here; its unique reputation in the history of cinema is simply hard to ignore.

Axial Alignment of the Camera/Spectator

This is the linchpin of Hou's stylistic system. Early in the film, the director introduces various settings with specific camera angles. These angles form an axis to which the camera will return throughout the film. Depending on the axis, the camera will either be irrevocably locked into that view or it will pan from one axis to another. More simply put, whenever Hou returns to a location he uses the identical angle, the same view. He does not use the same shot, however, because the camera is positioned at various points along that axis.

An excellent example is the ambush along a country road (see fig. 3). The principle at work is obvious because the scene is split into two long takes; the only camera movement involves slight reframings. The first shot shows the second brother waiting near the camera, leisurely smoking a cigarette. This defines the axis, which runs down the road to a few houses where some carriages arrive. The brother tosses his cigarette and walks slowly toward the carriages. As he leaves the camera, the Japanese sword in one hand suddenly becomes visible and the scene is transformed with a foreboding of menacing violence. When he breaks into a run and begins fighting, the second shot jumps backward and above the first camera position, *yet essentially maintains the same camera axis.*

Any citizen of the cinema world knows that a standard approach to this kind of fight scene would enhance the violence through as many shots—taken from as many angles—as possible. Indeed, Hong Kong cinema takes this principle to its natural end. This scene obeys a different set of rules. At other settings in *City of Sadness,* this principle is always at work, though in much more subtle ways because of Hou's use of sequence shots. A setting becomes intimately familiar as the view of it is repeated over the course of the film.

The two images in fig. 4 represent the first and last images of the hospital lobby. The image on the left sets up an axis that runs the length of the long lobby and occurs near the beginning of the film. Every subsequent shot of the lobby is located somewhere along this axis, moving back and forth depending on the scene. These shots are all static long shots (the only tracking shot of the film moves laterally). Interestingly enough, the first and last views

Fig. 3. This scene features two long takes photographed from the same axis. When the attack begins Hou defies generic expectations and backs away from the violence, shooting essentially from the same camera axis.

Fig. 4. The top shot is the first view of the hospital entranceway. It establishes an axis that the camera moves back and forth on throughout the film. Curiously, the final shot (on the bottom) returns to the camera position of the first.

of the entrance use exactly the same camera positioning—so far back on the axis that the camera is in a darkened backroom.

To give some sense of how extensive this is, the list below contains the eight predefined axes used by the seventeen shots of the film's most extraordinary sequence. In the space of fifteen minutes, we see the family through the death of the Oldest Son, his funeral, the marriage of Wen-ching (Youngest Son) and Hinomi, the birth of their son, and finally the death of Hinomi's brother. These axes are:

- *Shrine room axis:* shots 6, 8, 9; used twenty times in the film
- *Bar hallway axis:* shot 1; repeated twice
- *Light table and hallway axis:* shots 11, 16; repeated five times
- *Street market axis:* shot 10; repeated twice
- *Dinner table and bedroom axis:* shots 12, 15, 17; repeated fourteen times
- *Distant bay axis:* shot 14; repeated three times
- *Funeral axis:* shots 3, 4; repeated twice
- *Hospital entrance axis:* shot 13; repeated eight times

This principle of restricting the camera to a predefined axis is directly related to other aspects of Hou's style in exceedingly complicated ways. If the stageline and the proscenium effect it creates is the cornerstone of classical montage—the imaginary line that organizes all cinematic space—then the camera axis replaces that organizing function in Hou's narrative system. As we demonstrate below, this "uncinematic" shooting strategy produces playful variations of mise-en-scène and amplifies the powerful impact of the film's violence.

One of Hou's assistant directors, Angelika Wang, tells a revealing story related to Hou's approach. She said that after a set was built, and before the director and cinematographer arrived on the scene, the crew would gather on the set and place bets on which axis the director would place his camera on. Even Hou was surprised to hear this story.

Geometricization of Space

Hou's shots often display a spectacular geometricization of the mise-en-scène, revealing a fascination with graphic play. For example, in the main house the wall of windowpanes divides the movie screen into a field of rectangles (fig. 5). This view recurs throughout the film, often with people both in front of

Fig. 5. Hou's shots often display a spectacular geometricization of the mise-en-scène, revealing a fascination for graphic play.

and behind the windows. He often foregrounds the intersecting lines of the windows and doorways by placing the characters behind them. The action continues smoothly while the composition undergoes rather extreme stylization, a stylization that can be appreciated in and of itself. In other rooms of the same house, windows are decorated with stained glass diamond patterns. These diamonds often provide the backdrop for dinners and discussions, and shift from one pattern to another depending on the room. Besides signaling location, they function on a level of graphic play from one scene to the next, signaling an appreciation of the frame as pure composition—a predilection that Hou shares with Japanese director Ozu Yasujiro.

This stylized mise-en-scène may be found in Hou's earlier films as well. In these films, it is easily attributable to the Japanese architecture, which is naturally divided into squares and rectangles. However, by virtue of his consistency, it becomes clear that Hou is composing his shots with an unusual sophistication and under quite different rules. Hou's composition constantly emphasizes the geometry of the architecture. Throughout the director's work, human characters compete with squares, rectangles, and hexagons for attention. Finally, the geometricization of space in *Daughter of the Nile* (Ni luo he nu'er 尼羅河女兒, 1987), one of Hou's most formally beautiful works, is more extreme than *City of Sadness;* there is no teleology at work in Hou's oeuvre, only an orientation toward the perfectly refined composition and stylization.

Camera Movement

Nearly all camera movement in Hou's cinema occurs in takes up to several minutes long. The few pans in this film generally sweep from one axis to another, from one familiar tableau to the next. Furthermore, in *City of Sadness* the camera position moves in the course of a shot only once: a slow lateral tracking shot when an old woman arrives at a meeting to mediate a dispute. The slow track splits a long take into two distinct tableaux (a hallway and a meeting room). Finally, camera movement is motivated by the actions of characters, so that despite this constant reframing Hou's films contain an overwhelming sense of stillness. This stylistic effect greatly empowers Hou's thematic use of still photography, which we discuss below. In fact, the style of the film is actually identified with still photography: the only point of view shots in the film are connected to the look of Wen-ching's camera, for example when he shoots a farewell photograph of a teacher and his students.

Of all of Hou's films, *City of Sadness* is probably the most severe in its restriction of camera movement. In subsequent films, he uses constant reframing, as well as pans that disregard the camera axes he used in previous scenes.

Delimitation of the Frame

Hou enhances the graphic possibilities of composition through the delimitation of the frame, another aspect of mise-en-scène directly linked to his restricting the camera to predefined axes and the geometricization of space. Figure 6 shows two striking examples from *Summer at Grandpa's*. Both are views repeated throughout the film. They are photographed using 180-degree jumps over a staircase landing. The image on the top shows the landing cutting down the usable space for actors to the top half, and emphasizes the geometric qualities of the hexagonal window in the background. For the image on the bottom Hou pares down the narrative space to a tiny window.

The most striking example from *City of Sadness* is the hospital lobby of (see all the shots using this setting in fig. 8). The space is divided into four areas: the lobby itself, the contiguous rooms offscreen, the stairway outside the entrance, and a back room that the camera enters and departs. The graceful, arched doorway creates a second frame inside the film frame, and contains a partially eclipsed stairway that people ascend and descend, emphasizing the offscreen space above the top edge. At several points, the camera returns to the hospital lobby and is placed back in a darkened room; the dark walls of the doorway delimit the visible dimensions of the movie screen into an area one-sixth of its normal size, in effect creating a third frame. Furthermore, it is now a nearly perfect square. Not only does the space of *City of Sadness* become fractured into a graphic plane, but the size and shape of the screen itself (at least what is available to the narrative) varies. Hou's other films use this frame-within-a-frame composition. From these examples, it becomes particularly clear that this works in tandem with geometricization to emphasize the graphic qualities of the image.

Ellipsis (and the Long Take)/Control (and Freedom)

Because of the long take's close association with the theoretical assumptions of neorealism, any subsequent use of it makes for a deceiving representation of the real by duplicating the original mistakes of the neorealists. Most cru-

Fig. 6. An extreme example of the delimitation of space from *Summer at Grandpa's*.

cially, they emphasized the synthetic qualities of the long take while ignoring the contradictions posed by the inevitable use of ellipsis. To look at the temporal gaps between takes (of long or any length) is to acknowledge the artificial, constructed nature of the long take style. Thus, when Hou's critics point out his "realistic" use of the long take, they inevitably refer to his style in terms of realism, rather than stylization and overt control.

By way of contrast, we will emphasize the consciously creative use of ellipsis in relation to the long take. For example, when the second brother insults a rival gang member in the club's restroom and a fight breaks out, it seems to be completely contained in a sequence shot because the second shot is of a card game in what appears to be a different time and place. However, a few long beats after the beginning of the second shot, the fight erupts into the room and is broken up; the second brother lies wounded in his elder brother's arms. Once again, the next (third) shot seems to begin a new sequence as the rival gang's boss walks down a corridor, but the sounds of a fight fade into the background and now older brother bursts into the hallway only to be shot. The endings of both the first and second shots appear to contain an ending; however, they actually conceal an undecidable ellipsis that becomes evident only in retrospect. Every aperture seems to contain a surprise.

By making the temporal gaps between sequence shots of indeterminate length, Hou forces a curious instability into the image. One is never confident in the temporal or spatial coordinates at the beginning of a shot, forcing the spectator to rely heavily on the previous sequence shot until the who, what, when, and where of a shot/sequence is established. This constant need to ground a sequence shot in what came before makes elements of one shot's time, space, narrative, and mood bleed into the next. Hou is well aware of this effect: "When I cut between scenes, I try to allow the unfinished atmosphere of the last shot to continue into the next" (David Kehr, "Director Makes Ordinary Life Extraordinary"). This has the effect of smoothing out the cuts between shots, making the film a distinctly amorphous experience. This plays into idealizations of the long take aesthetic as closer to reality, as a method that grants a measure of freedom to both the spectator and the actors (nonactors who are allowed to improvise their own dialogue). However, this effect is created by embedding the long take in a controlling, far from obvious structure, creating a subtle dialectic between freedom and control.

Long Shot/Close-up

In *City of Sadness,* the closest Hou's camera approaches any character is from the chest up, what would probably be defined a medium close-up. It is a physical distance that translates into an emotional one as well. However, Hou's films can be quite moving, and the lack of close-ups is (surprisingly enough) one of the reasons.

Medium close-ups of single characters are close enough to make facial expressions legible, but by keeping the camera away from the action, long shots emphasize the context among characters. By extension, this occasionally reflects a cultural emphasis on the family before the individual, deriving, in the last instance, from a long history of Confucian thought. This suggests that in American movies, our cultural obsession with individuality translates into a cinematic singling out by means of the close-up; narrative focus on a hero is complemented by the mise-en-scène. *City of Sadness* presents an alternative approach to mise-en-scène where, more often than not, the characters are seen (in long shot) in the context of other family members. In fact, the only true close-up of the film is of a photograph Wen-ching is touching up: a family portrait. Hou compounds his visual orientation toward the plural by diffusing the narrative attention among a number of characters. As in most of his other films, it is difficult to decide who the primary character is.

According to Hou, he began using long shots to cover for his nonprofessional actors. At the same time, he asserts that the long shot—combined with the long take—produces a special kind of image: "I'm not using the long shot just for the sake of the actors. A screen holding a long shot has a certain kind of tension, and for this you can't find an alternative method to substitute. I realize I am confronted with a contradiction here" (Mart Dominic and Peter Delpeut, "A Man Must Be Greater Than His Films," 16). It is difficult to provide an example of this effect, since it relies heavily on the accumulation of emotional resonance from shot to shot. At the same time, moving in for the close-up when Hinomi and Wen-ching learn of Hiromi's death is unthinkable. Nothing is more devastating than watching nearly three minutes of their baby crawling around, oblivious to their tragedy (see fig. 20 in chapter 4). Likewise, the palpable tension in Hou's long shots is crucial for energizing offscreen space and the violence it just barely contains.

Revelation of Spatial Relationships

Hou constructs his cinematic space through gradual, incremental revelation. Since each view is locked into a predefined axis, the overall sense of space builds slowly over the course of the film. At times, spaces that seem like separate locations are suddenly revealed to be adjacent. Only by actively perceiving visual cues can the spectator construct a more complex sense of the relationships between spaces. These visual cues consist of pans from one axis to another, as well as props or landmarks acting as spatial anchors that may be seen from more than one axis. The spatial relationship for two of the most highly used spaces in the film—the main entranceway with its porcelain vase and the shrine room—is hazy at best. The spectator knows they are in the same house; however, only late in the film does a discreet cut from one long take to another reveal they are adjacent rooms. Both spaces are familiar because Hou always uses the same camera angle whenever he returns to each room; that they are adjacent is evident only when Eldest Brother walks from one room to the other.

In this way, initially fragmented space is incrementally homogenized, until one should have a sense of any set's layout by the end of the film. Hou's gradual revelation of space, the variation from view to view as the camera is placed at different points along its axes, and the concomitant play of graphic forms serve to unify the film structurally while maintaining a quality of indeterminacy and fragmentation that contributes to the film's dialogical properties.

Transitional Spaces

Hou's use of transitional shots with vague connections to the diegesis prompts some critics to make comparisons to Japanese director Ozu Yasujiro (although, as we argue below, this comparison is dubious). Generally, these transitions are single long takes and consist of long shots of natural settings, such as the bay, the mountains, or a road switchbacking up a hillside. They provide a gentle punctuation between scenes, a little space to pause that adds to the film's measured rhythm and quiet atmosphere. In terms of narration, they function in a variety of ways. The road transition usually occurs when a character begins a trip. The view of the bay defines the setting of Kee-lung, where the February 28 massacre began. They are also related to Hou's creative use of ellipsis, for few of the shots are temporally marked. They imply some indeterminate passing of time, but it is rarely clear how much.

Shot-Reverse Shot

One of the most surprising restrictions Hou imposes on himself is his minimal use of the shot-reverse shot. Other aspects of his style factor in here—the long take, the refusal of the close-up—testifying to the interconnectedness of all these.

City of Sadness contains only six moments that could be considered the shot-reverse shot figure. Most of these are simply perfect 90-degree shifts around a dinner table, but as exceptions the shot-reverse shots often come at strategic moments that integrate other aspects of his style. A significant instance of this in *City of Sadness* is found in the wedding scene, which is particularly fascinating for formal reasons. Containing four long takes, this sequence is staged "incorrectly" by the standards of classical style, but it obeys the rules we have been discussing for Hou's films. The shot plan in figure 7 shows the positioning of the camera for each shot.

The wedding party enters the room and begins the ceremony on the other side of the glass wall (shot 1); the couple faces the shrine, with their backs toward the camera. A reverse shot shows a "perfectly" composed view of the couple standing before the altar (shot 2). Because it is both a reverse shot and a closer view of the couple, the shot initially seems like a typical strategy for singling out protagonists, for encouraging our identification with them. However, every time the couple bows they drop nearly completely below the frame, revealing their family overseeing the ceremony in the background. The mundane reverse shot turns out to be a typical shot emphasizing the context of the family.

This is, in turn, followed by another reverse shot of the bowing couple, yet containing rather odd, "improper" composition (shot 3). Because shot 2 shows the bride and groom facing the left-hand side of the frame, classical rules would dictate that the reverse shot over their shoulders would basically duplicate the eye line: they would be placed on the right, looking left into the center of the frame. However, while shot 3 reverses the angle to a view of the couple's backs, it is nudged to the right so that the groom is now edging into offscreen space and the bride looks left at the side of the frame. In the center of the frame the patriarch of the family sits, watching the proceedings with approval.

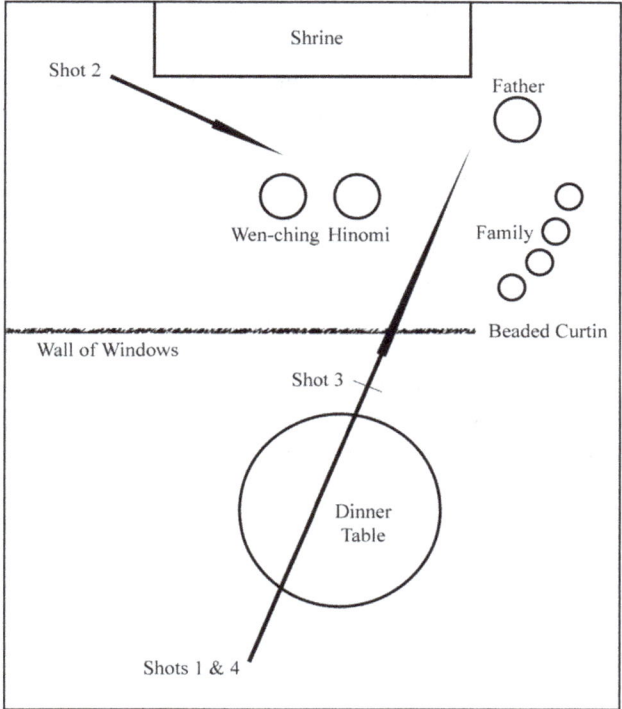

Fig. 7. Containing four long takes, this sequence is staged "incorrectly" by the standards of classical style, but it obeys the rules of Hou's cinema.

This reverse shot is "wrong" in that the camera is turned slightly too far to the right (thus cutting off the groom and allowing no on-screen space for the bride to look into); a classically composed shot would put the father to the left of the couple (in the space they face). On the other hand, it is quite correct in the context of Hou's style in two ways. First, it emphasizes the domestic and familial circumstances in which the action takes place. The mise-en-scène focuses our attention on the father and his new daughter-in-law, expanding the narrative scope of the wedding to include the entire family; in other words, it emphasizes context rather than the individual.

A second, more compelling, reason it is not "wrong" relates to Hou's peculiar penchant for snapping the camera onto the same axis every time he returns to a set. The reverse shot that follows shot 2 ignores the needs of classical narrative that would dictate we see the two main characters framed in a similar (centered) manner from each angle. Instead, it responds to Hou's own rules, locking into the axis defined by shot 1, which "naturally" relegates the groom to offscreen space and the bride to the left-hand side of the frame. Furthermore, shot 4, the last shot of the scene, replicates the view of shot 1 and represents a perfect jump backward along the axis from shot 3. This scene violates the classical sense of narrative space, while it obeys the laws of editing intrinsic to Hou's style.

Repetition

This is where all of the aspects of Hou's style coalesce to form a wellspring of affective power. Because the camera sits on various points of an axis, the same view is repeated over and over through the film. The more important the space, the more often its image is repeated. This is responsible for much of the emotional effectiveness of Hou's style because the shots come to resonate, both subtly and powerfully, with each other. As a view is repeated, a residue of action and emotion builds.

For example, consider the view of the hospital hallway (fig. 8). Here we see a band marching down the outside steps during the celebration of Japan's defeat. Long separated friends reunite beneath its graceful, arched entrance. When the political situation turns sour and the violence of the February 28 Incident begins, wounded Chinese are carried through its portal . . . followed by an angry mob of Taiwanese. Later, we hear the radio broadcast of the Nationalist leader echo through the halls, assuring the country—with bold hypocrisy—that nothing is wrong. Not long after that, Hinomi crosses

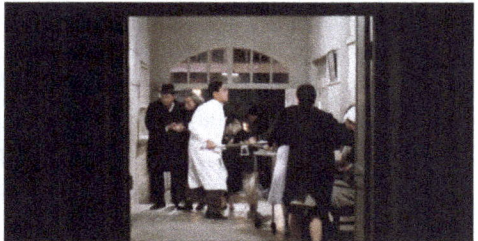

Fig. 8. Repeated constantly throughout the film, shots of the hospital lobby come to resonate, both subtly and powerfully, against each other. A residue of action and emotion builds as a view is repeated.

the hospital's threshold to give birth to her son, and the emotions and memories associated with all this life, death, and pain coalesce.

The view of the shrine is one of the most highly charged in the film because of this narrative and visual repetition. The first time we see it, a celebration for the opening of the new family business is under way. After that, it is repeated in nineteen long takes, serving as the site of weddings, scoldings, feasts, reunions, and the mending of emotional and physical wounds. The table in the foreground serves as the site of countless meals, and tallies the toll the political sea changes take on the family. Fewer and fewer sons are alive to share meals, and in the devastating penultimate shot of the film only the patriarch and his shell-shocked son survive to eat together. As for the rest of the family, their absence is their presence thanks to this constant, poignant repetition.

This emotional residue is capable of charging "empty" shots as well: the last image of the film is simply the staid Chinese vase sitting below the diamonds of stained glass. Nothing happens. But the events that echo throughout that space infuse it with a quiet sadness.

The broad contrasts that these repetitions involve would be clumsy and ineffective had they been traditionally juxtaposed by means of montage. Instead, by virtue of their common placement in nearly identical mise-en-scène, they resonate across the vast temporal reaches of the narrative.

Violence . . . Seen and Unseen

In one of the most astounding scenes of *City of Sadness,* Wen-ching sits in prison (fig. 9). KMT guards open the door and brusquely take a few men away. As their footsteps echo down what sounds like a long hallway, the camera lingers on the deaf Wen-ching, who broods silently behind a barred window. The footsteps stop, followed by the report of gunfire.

This execution—visceral for its suddenness and invisibility—does not register on Wen-ching's handicapped body; he watched them go, but could not hear them die. It makes the next scene all the more disturbing, for the same soldiers return and take Wen-ching into the troubling offscreen space. This scene is the purest example of the (indirect) representation of violence in Hou's films.

The centrality of this representation of violence, particularly in relation to Hou's particular stylistic system and his narration of the nation, will concern this section of our analysis. This curiously reserved approach to vio-

Fig. 9. In one of the most astounding scenes of *City of Sadness*, Wen-ching sits in prison as KMT guards brusquely take a few men away. He cannot hear their receding footsteps or the sound of gunfire that follows.

lence informs all of Hou's films. It is radically different than the ballet-like stylization of Hong Kong films, the cultivated precision of Japanese cinematic swordplay, or American cinema's spectacularization and fetishization of violence through the use of close-ups, rapid cutting, realistic makeup, and special effects. Hou tends to pull away from the sometimes savage acts of his stories and show them from a distance.

This reticent approach is taken to an extreme in *City of Sadness,* where most of the acts of violence are pushed far away from the camera—often offscreen. When mobs of Taiwanese start beating Chinese in the wake of the February 28 Incident, we see fights in the distance, which are then shoved into the background in the shot of Hinoe watching in disbelief; then the violence is pushed entirely offscreen in the subsequent shot.

In another scene of retribution (fig. 3), Second Brother stands on a country lane, cut off from the waist down by the bottom edge of the frame (we do not yet realize that he's hiding something in the offscreen space). Carriages arrive in the distance; when Second Brother runs toward them, the Japanese sword he was holding offscreen comes into view. We watch as he and his friends attack the men from the carriage in extreme long shot, moving on- and offscreen as they run behind the tall grass and buildings.

This strategic placement of violence just beyond sight may be found in other Taiwanese films. In "Hou Hsiao-hsien and Narrative Space," Abé Mark Nornes has argued that Edward Yang's delegation of violence to offscreen spaces serves as an organizing function. It should be remembered that Hou and Yang have worked closely in the profilmic spaces, both behind and before the camera. Indeed, Hou's unusual portrayal of violent acts in extreme long shots is somewhat reminiscent of the fight on the lonely road at the end of Edward Yang's *Taipei Story.* Here Hou himself (acting in the main role) is attacked and receives a stab wound that causes his character's death.

At the same time, Hou also articulates this approach with other aspects of his style, making the use of offscreen violence his own. For example, in one of the first scenes of conflict, a knife fight breaks out in the nightclub's hallway. Hou cuts in midfight to what appears to be one of his poetic transitional shots, which we have come to expect: a pair of rickshaws pull up to a peaceful town in extreme long shot. By this time we have learned that these pretty land- and cityscapes mark the ends of scenes and contain undecidable ellipses in time. A man emerges from one of the rickshaws and enters a building, while villagers mill around an open area gossiping. Thirty seconds into this minute-long shot, the fight from the previous scene bursts into the open area—into on-screen space. Hou masterfully builds up our expectations for a poetic transition shot introduced by a typically undecidable ellipsis, only to reveal that there was no temporal gap between the shots, that there was neither transition nor ellipsis.

Since the most violent act of the film, the February 28 Incident itself, occurs offscreen, it is crucial to examine more closely this relationship between violence and space. In this respect, Marsha Kinder's elaboration of the iterative in cinema, in "The Subversive Potential of the Pseudo-Iterative," is useful to understanding how this approach to violence relates to the film's politics. The iterative refers to stating once that which happened multiple times. All films contain both iterative and singulative aspects. The classical style tends to emphasize its singulative characters, while relegating iterative aspects to mere background. On the other hand, a style like neorealism (or the early Taiwan New Cinema, for that matter) foregrounds the slippage between the two, because it is the typicality of its narrative that is important. The troubles of Vittorio De Sica's singulative bicycle thief, for example, are meant to evoke the common experience of the entire nation's poor.

In like manner, there is a constant, prominent slippage between the singulative family at the center of Hou's narrative and the collective experience of Taiwanese between the twin pressures of the Japanese and the Nationalists. While a typical Hollywood film would focus on the family to the exclusion of larger political issues, *City of Sadness* centers on a single family to speak for every family, or the nation as family. The movement from the singular experience of the family to other levels often occurs in the mise-en-scène. Kinder notes, "The interplay between singulative event and the paradigm it represents is frequently played out spatially in terms of foreground and background" (7). An example in *City of Sadness* would be the scene mentioned above with Hinoe at the railway station. After Hinoe watches the indiscriminate beatings in the distance, the sequence ends with Wen-ching becoming the focus of a mob's wrath.

Furthermore, Hou's style offers a further, more peculiar, space of the iterative. Here the iterative is played out in terms of on- and offscreen space. In the prison scene we described at the beginning of this section, Wen-ching watches two anonymous men walk into offscreen space to their deaths, and then shortly thereafter he follows them down the same hallway. Throughout the film, we hear the seemingly endless repetition of "So and so has been arrested. So and so has disappeared," over and over again. We see incidents of mob rule, police roundups, and searches as they affect the singulative Lin family; at the same time, the sounds of these types of violence performed against other families form a sonic backdrop as constant as a musical score.

By initiating violence against the main characters onscreen, then relegating paradigmatic violence to the offscreen spaces, Hou cultivates the oppressive sense that this is happening across the entire island, affecting hundreds of thousands of families.

We would also argue that extratextual factors enter into the iterative. It must be remembered that every family in Taiwan has stories about how this turbulent time affected their own family. This personal history certainly constitutes a central reading code for the film; what happens to the Lin family is read through the experience of one's own family memories and, by extension, the nation as a whole.

Hou has repeatedly claimed he did not set out to make a "political" movie, yet the decision to make a film about this period has wide-ranging political implications. Until *City of Sadness* was released, the subject of the February 28 Incident was strictly taboo and repressed from public discourse. Hou ran the risk of censorship, and strategically showed the film abroad before releasing it in Taiwan. After the Venice Film Festival prize, the threat of government censorship quickly died. Upon its release, it generated a healthy, furious debate, which Hou surely foresaw. He was doomed to satisfy no one, and he did not. The immigrants from the mainland and their descendants felt the movie let the Japanese off scot free, while portraying the actions of the KMT unfairly. Taiwanese, on the other hand, still reeling from the massacre of 2.28 and its bloody retributions, felt betrayed. They point out that the incident itself occurs offscreen, and that much of the violence shown is initiated by Taiwanese against mainlanders.

Hou both evades and addresses these issues through the use of the iterative and offscreen violence. Being the first media figure to broach the subject of the massacre, Hou was under enormous pressure in terms of how to represent the previously unrepresentable. Like other filmmakers working under conditions restricting their expression (for example, Kamei Fumio in wartime Japan, John Huston in wartime America, Sergei Paradjanov in the Soviet Union), Hou chose to speak indirectly. Pushing the most sensitive violence to the offscreen spaces—and multiplying the victims of that violence by invocation of the iterative—allowed Hou to bring this repressed, formative moment in the history of the nation into the open for the people in Taiwan to reflect upon its meaning for today.

While this film was in production, the government of Taiwan was containing social and political unrest in a high-handed way, despite the lifting of martial law. The film does not go for the jugular, but it certainly promoted movement toward healthy dialogue and freedom of expression. Taiwanese cinema presents a situation we've seen in many countries emerging from long periods of censorship and repression, adopting an ambiguous stance in the face of the authorities' cold, pedagogical clarity. It is into this ambiguous space, through a quirk of timing, that the events of June 4, 1989, in Beijing inserted themselves, perhaps extending the iterative across space and time, for it was impossible to watch Hou's film without thinking that Beijing was also a *City of Sadness*.

Hou and Ozu

While Hou Hsiao-hsien (1947–) and Ozu Yasujiro (1903–1963) are undoubtedly two of the great masters of world cinema, they are radically different directors. This did not stop many early critics from making facile comparisons, or even claiming that the Japanese director influenced Hou. This section investigates these claims to winnow out their differences as well as their similarities.

Stylistic Predilections

> [*A Summer at Grandpa's*] is his most Ozu-like film, with overtones of works like *Ohayo* and even of *Tokyo Story.* The opening scene, a prelude in which newly graduated children sing farewell to their old school, works in the same way as the emotional climax of *Tokyo Story,* in which the daughter glances at the watch just given her by her aunt and the sound of the children's singing carries into the next shot.
>
> —Alan Stanbrook, "The Worlds of Hou Hsiao-hsien"

> At the end of [*A Summer at Grandpa's*], the quiet appearance of the grandfather and grandmother on the bridge makes one remember Ozu's *Tokyo Story.*
>
> —Chiao Hsiung-ping, "A Summer at Grandpa's"

The early sequences, depicting the repatriation of the occupying Japanese after 1945, even look Japanese. The beautiful scene which is shot in the same way by an Ozu or a Mizoguchi in the 1950s. And it is not just a matter of influence. Hou has always maintained that the Ozu flavour many have found in his work is coincidental because at the time it was first remarked upon, he had never seen an Ozu film. Perhaps; but Ozu, after all, was part of the Japanese cultural heritage and for more than fifty years Taiwanese life was imbued with it. Hou may have arrived after the Japanese had left the island, but their legacy lingered on.

—Alan Stanbrook, "The Worlds of Hou Hsiao-hsien"

[Mr. Hou's] *Summer at Grandpa's* . . . looked as if it were the director's "Truffaut film." *Daughter of the Nile* evokes the alienated mood of the early features by France's Jean-Luc Godard, while Mr. Hou's use of the camera suggests that he is an appreciative student of Japan's Ozu Yasujiro, the poet laureate of graceful resignation. Mr. Hou has studied the work of the masters and borrowed their methods and manners to express feelings that, though authentic and true, ultimately seem secondhand because his film language isn't his own.

—Vincent Canby, "Why Some Movies Don't Travel Well"

Hou Hsiao-hsien favours the use of motifs, similar to those "punctuation marks" that are such a marked feature of Ozu's films.

—Alan Stanbrook, "The Worlds of Hou Hsiao-hsien"

Hasumi: "Your films are often said to be Ozu-like, but I disagree completely. . . . Rather, the sensitivity of your scenes have a European, as opposed to an American or Hollywood feel. Are you at all conscious of this in any way?"

Hou: "I've never thought of that. On the other hand, since I was small and in my student days, the movies I saw were, more than anything, American. For a long time, it was impossible to see European films in Taiwan. Last year there was a film festival in Taiwan, and there was an international section. At that time, I saw a comparatively large number of foreign films. So whenever that kind of thing is said, it feels strange."

—Hasumi Shigehiko, "I Think Making a Scene Is, in the Final Instance, Intuition"

Ozu always used the family as a backdrop. . . . I saw many of Ozu's films, and in most of them a daughter gets married. These events take place in different periods and each is shown from a different perspective and a different context. That's a very difficult challenge for an artist because you can't film the same theme repeatedly without great self-confidence. . . . Ozu's films were a revelation to me. I used to think my observations and insight into the human condition were very objective, but I can't compare with Ozu.

—Hou Hsiao-hsien, on the occasion
of the thirty-year anniversary of Ozu's death

Ozu Yasujiro's name is invoked regularly in discussions of Hou in both Taiwan and Japan, and among Western critics as well. As with neorealism it is a relationship begging for clarification. Few critics comparing the two directors attempted any real close analysis. They tended to base their comparisons on misunderstandings of both directors' narrative strategies and on cultural essentializations (of self, other, or both). In fact, Hou did not see Ozu's work until the late 1980s, after he already demonstrated his own peculiar approach to narration in films such as *The Boys from Fengkuei* and *The Time to Live and the Time to Die*.

Ozu may very well be a useful reference point for thinking about Hou's achievement. It is easy to cite a few general areas of overlap: minimalism, a predilection for unusual self-restraint and systematization, as well as a fascination for the graphic qualities of the image. When he finally saw Ozu's work he found a kindred spirit. This helps explain the subtle homage to Ozu in Hou's 1995 *Good Men, Good Women* (Haonan haonü 好男好女; see fig. 10). In one

Fig. 10. Late in his career, Hou expressed his admiration for Ozu in a televisual homage to *Late Spring* in a complex long take featuring both reframing and tracking.

scene the main character has a television playing in the background, and the film is Ozu's masterpiece *Late Spring* (Banshun 晩春, 1949).

However, to posit influences is misleading to say the least. Uncovering the shaky basis for the Ozu = Hou comparison turns us to the reception context for Hou's work, particularly his vigorous promotion by a handful of powerful Western critics and his enthusiastic fans in Japan. These two groups tend to include Ozu as a vector of their approach to Hou, hinting at a neocolonial postmodernism (for the Japanese audiences and media industry) or orientalism (for many Western critics who painstakingly search for some ideal pan-Asian representative).

Self-Restraint

Ozu, like Hou, was anything but flashy. Indeed, for most critics who connect the two directors, this vague sense of self-restraint covering both their films probably constitutes the main basis for comparison. For Ozu, any effects that interfered with his own ideas about composition were cast away; he never zoomed and used only one dissolve (in the 1930 *Life of an Office Worker* [Kaishain seikatsu 会社員生活]). Because he also subordinated camera movement to composition, he did not use pans because they disturbed his framing. The few tracking shots he staged were designed to maintain a static composition (by moving along a road with a character, for example). When Ozu began shooting in color, he did away with camera movement altogether. As a general comparison, Hou and Ozu seem quite similar in terms of their self-restraint. However, when one looks at specifics the comparison breaks down. Most of Hou's shots involve slight reframings, despite their apparent stillness. He occasionally trucks his camera, but unlike Ozu he does not attempt to maintain the same composition throughout the pan. Hou may show proclivities toward Ozu's approach to cinema, but he is by no means as rigorous.

Transitions

Both Ozu and Hou insert curious forms of transitions between scenes and sequences. In Ozu's case, they have been labeled "pillow shots" or "curtain shots" by various critics. Between scenes he would always place carefully framed shots of the surroundings to signal changes in setting, as well as for less scrutable reasons. Basically a hybrid of the cutaway and the placement shot, they are considered unusual for being quite extended, and apparently motivated primarily by graphic composition and pacing. Many critics have noted what seems to be a suspension of narration in Ozu's transitions—to the point that some have called them extradiegetic. While Hou's transitions evoke similar effects, a notable difference is that Hou's are usually single shots. Ozu's transitions involve multiple shots, and he often pivots around objects in the frame from shot to shot. In a transition near the beginning of *Floating Weeds* (Ukigusa 浮草, 1959) the camera revolves around a lighthouse, objects with the name of an acting troupe (a poster and banners), buildings, and people. Ozu's transitions often involve such playful graphic matching of shapes and spaces through a series of shots, but Hou appears more interested in using his long-take transitions to create mood and narrative "breathing space."

Low Angles

Ozu's signature feature is the low angle, which is usually (but not always) shot with a camera set close to the ground. Every shot of the film uses it. While many writers have identified it as the point of view of a child, a dog, a god, or a person sitting Japanese style on tatami mats, David Bordwell, in *Ozu and the Poetics of Cinema,* convincingly argues that its position is actually proportional, meaning the height always changes as long as it stays lower than the object being shot. This makes all the lines in the frame follow generally the same pattern from shot to shot.

Hou does place his camera close to the ground at times, but this is almost exclusively in scenes set inside Japanese architecture. As a former Japanese colony, Taiwan has had many Japanese style buildings, or rooms with tatami floors. In *City of Sadness* Wen-ching's home has several of these rooms, and scenes set here use a camera relatively close to the ground. Because people sit on the floor in these spaces, it only makes sense to lower the camera so it does not look down on them. In this sense, Hou is actually similar to most Japanese directors, who also place the camera at a low angle when shooting in traditional Japanese spaces.

360-Degree Spaces

Ozu's most radical departure from classical style was his use of 360-degree space. By convention, Hollywood style dictates that the camera should stay within a 180-degree space to one side of the action. It is felt this will provide proper "screen direction" and a sense of homogeneous space. Ozu's camera, on the other hand, orbits around the characters in a circle, using all 360 degrees. This can be found easily in any Ozu film. This produces a number of unusual effects that the classical style finds undesirable, such as graphic matching, but Ozu's melodramas are so compelling that the engrossed spectator does not find them disrupting. When Hou breaks his scenes into more than one shot, he often shifts the camera a clean 45-degrees to one side (often around a table). However, these instances are extremely unusual and he generally sticks to the classical rule, leaving his camera on one side of the action.

Graphic Matching and Actors

An effect produced by Ozu's jumping over the stageline is that actors facing each other seem to look off in the same direction. Ozu exploited the graphic possibilities of this by placing people in identical positions between (as well as within) shots. Ozu also favored a sitting position with the actor's body "torqued" to face the camera. To many an actor's frustration, their bodies were treated as objects to be carefully manipulated within the frame, and their lines had to be delivered with a minimum of emoting and movement. Ozu pushed this "graphic matching" between shots to notorious extremes; it is not unusual to see props such as beer bottles seem to skitter across tables or move closer to the camera to preserve their size and screen position from shot to shot. This is one of the most distinct aspects of Ozu's style, and nothing close to it may be found in Hou's cinema—with the exception of *Café Lumière* (Kohii jiko 珈琲時光, 2003), his homage to the Japanese director.

We've seen how Hou uses a geometricization of space that creates images comparable to Ozu's indoor scenes. However, Ozu's graphic matching relies on regular and relatively rapid cutting, the use of many shots within and between scenes. Furthermore, as Bordwell has argued, the basis of Ozu's style is a modification of Hollywood's shot-reverse shot, a figure that is the exception to the rule in Hou's case. In fact, to our knowledge Ozu never used a sequence shot—he was surely disinclined to use them because they would interfere with graphic matching and other effects he loved.

Café Lumière *as Homage*

We can look to Hou Hsiao-hsien's *Café Lumière* for the director's own comment on his relationship to Ozu. This was a Shochiku production designed to celebrate the 100th birthday of the Japanese director. While they could have drawn on their own stable of reliable melodrama directors—for example, Yamada Yoji—someone at the studio had the good sensibility to bring in Hou Hsiao-hsien.

The result was pure Hou, with gestures to Ozu. The film starts with the old-style Shochiku logo in the Academy ratio the Japanese director shot in, followed by a train shot (fig. 11, upper right, an image that references Lumière as much as the Japanese director). The film's second shot (lower left) establishes an axis through the main character's apartment, and deploys a low camera angle that produces characteristically Ozu-like lines in the architecture. In a very long take, the character hangs wet clothing on a line, chatting on the phone about mundane matters of everyday life. She walks offscreen, leaving a clothesline full of clothes, an iconic Ozu image if there ever was one.

Then something very un-Ozu happens: the actor moves screen left and the camera pans with her (lower right). All this happens in the four-and-a-half minutes before the opening credits, and in only two shots.

Fig. 11. The opening shots from *Café Lumière* exhibit a dynamic between Ozu's style and Hou's style.

These shots encapsulate the film's dynamic between Ozu's style and Hou's style. The latter's homage to the Japanese master presents us with an intertwining of these two low-key approaches to cinematic narrative. The train shot was taken from an angle Ozu never would have considered. The second shot featured Ozu's iconography and camera positioning, but included pans and was nearly four minutes in length, a sequence in itself. There are strange ellipses, ubiquitous train travel and laundry, not to mention an (already pregnant) daughter who refuses marriage, but the similarities virtually end there. As James Udden writes, "One can argue that *Café Lumière* is true to the spirit of Ozu, but not the letter" (*No Man an Island,* 173).

Nation and Industry

This section on style has gone to great lengths to examine the manner in which Hou's direction departs from the codes of classical style (or other major paradigms of film style, for that matter). It is important to note that there are both industrial and cultural bases for the comparison as well. The nexus for all these concerns seems to be the film critics, who provide a reading protocol that depends on Ozu to measure Hou's difference to classical standards. Their desire to pin down Hou dovetails with larger ideological spheres, from neonationalism to orientalism depending upon the regional context.

By the late 1980s, Ozu's position as an "international auteur" and one of history's great film directors had been established through lengthy debates in Western film journals, books by Donald Richie and David Bordwell, and retrospectives throughout Europe, Asia, and the United States. In Japan, Ozu was the New Wave filmmakers' emblem for everything wrong with Japanese cinema. However, in the 1980s his reputation was resurrected, and he swiftly became canonized as one of Japan's greatest directors. This was largely due to the articles, lectures, speeches and books of Hasumi Shigehiko, one of Japan's most powerful scholars (and one-time president of Tokyo University), as well as the director's newfound recognition abroad. Nearly every year sees new works published on Ozu, and the works by Richie and Bordwell have even been translated into Japanese.

Hasumi was also one of the first writers to promote Taiwanese film in the early days of the Taiwan New Cinema (he also appears in a cameo in *Café Lumière*). For his own part, Hasumi was careful to avoid comparisons of Hou and Ozu, but other critics and audiences certainly were not. The connection helped pave the way for Hou's popularity, and by the time *City of Sadness* was released, all of Hou's previous films had been successfully distributed in Japan in theaters and home video. The theatrical releases included long runs in Tokyo's finest theaters, where one often found standing-room-only crowds day and night. In the early 1990s Hou was even hired by a chemical firm (Nippon Shokubai) to make a commercial for domestic broadcast; the ad offered all of the iconography of Hou's films—railroads, train tracks, laundry, long shots, and long takes—and certainly helped promote the release of several of Hou's films in Tokyo.

The fact that Hou's popularity would culminate in directing a television commercial—which would in turn be processed through a variety of media as news or promotion for his films—is emblematic of a shift in the discursive space of Heisei era Japan. At the end of the 1980s, Japanese turned their attention away from the West, and America in particular, and "rediscovered" Asia. Some critics spoke of a shift from a *sen* (line) to a *men* (surface) mentality, which is to say an abandoning of bilateral dependence upon the United States and a renewed consciousness of Japan's Asian connections and the economic and cultural riches of its neighbors. While the former evokes the rhetoric of World War II, such as *seimeisen* (lifeline), the new *men*-tality is more expansive. This new pan-Asian consciousness coincides with massive postmodern consumption cycles, which shrewdly exploit differences through swift commodification, consumption, and expulsion in favor of the ever-new. In fulfillment of vague calls to "internationalization" (*kokusaika*), Japanese business collected objects from around the world (including films) and brought them to its center. Yoshimoto Mitsuhiro has argued that underlying this metropolitan veneer is a surging neonationalism that commodifies the foreign by erasing any disturbing otherness. We may see this very operation at work in the Japanese critics' comparison of Hou and Ozu. By equating the two, they appeal to the postmodern pan-Asianism in circulation; some of the comparisons go so far as to point out Taiwan and Japan's historically close relationship, again erasing the more unpleasant aspects of this history in a vague neocolonial nostalgia.

Although critics outside of Japan turn to Ozu for quite different reasons, in their attempt to rationalize Hou's exceptional style they too turn to cultural explanations. For example, in a thoughtful commentary about how *City of Sadness* weighs upon his mind, Li Tuo ("Narratives of History in the Cinematography of Hou Xiaoxian," 815) contrasts Hou to Zhang Yimou, and ponders what a truly Chinese film style might look like:

> I once again think of *Raise the Red Lantern* (Da hong deng long ghao gao gua 大紅燈籠高高掛, 1991). It is evident that Zhang Yimou gave his all in making this film. . . . But if we peer through the dazzling light created by the various elements of this film's design to view the internal drama, anyone familiar with the traditions of Hollywood can easily see that this film is an exquisite copy of a Hollywood film. To copy Hollywood, of course, is not unusual. Film directors all over the world, motivated by all kinds of reasons, are doing just this. But if one puts a layer of artistic Oriental wrapping on the exterior of this copy and therefore believes one has created a Chinese film, then we can consult Hou Hsiao-hsien's film to raise a question: in whose eyes is *Raise the Red Lantern* a Chinese film?

He suggests that the loose narration of *City of Sadness* may provide a route to define what a Chinese film style might look like, but leaves the difficult task of specificity to future writing or other industrious critics. Formulating the difference is relatively easy; explaining it is something else again. Some Western critics have not shied away. In her description of a visit to the *City of Sadness* set, Georgia Brown writes in "Island in the Mainstream":

> Sometimes a figure sits in the middle distance, internally absorbed, while in the rest of the frame, various others are in motion, carrying on some mundane business, creating a Taoist-Confucian dialectic between depth and surface, passive and active. The effect also suggests the mind's internal play, tiers of experience, worlds within worlds.

This brand of orientalist mystification is typical, and one senses it in many of the comparisons between Hou and Ozu. For Western critics, the two directors share some kind of Asian sensibility that translates into their films (by virtue of colonial legacies or vague tropes of Asian sensibility). For Japanese, it is this and more; the popularity of both Hou and Ozu coincides with a resurgence of nationalism paired with intense postmodern consumption and appropriation of Japan's Asian others and thus, the fact that all his work is available in every format—including television commercials—should not be surprising.

In any case, the link to Ozu has proven fruitful for promoting Hou's films. The prestige of Ozu as one of film history's great auteurs evidently rubbed off on Hou. Combined with tropes of nationhood, Asian affiliation, and Chinese-ness, Hou's difference is tenuously grasped, celebrated, commodified, and consumed. Now is the time to move on to new perspectives.

3 / Sound/Writing/Photography

City of Sadness is remarkably rich with modes of representation, particularly still photography, sound recording, and various kinds of handwriting. Built into the fabric of the film's narration, they add layers of meaning that defy an easy, transparent telling of history, contesting the clarity of Nationalist historiography.

The reception of *City of Sadness* in Taiwan itself included an attempt to mount a counterargument against the film. Many of these articles are collected in a book entitled *Death of the New Cinema*. These writers suggest that the ambiguous narrative space and time, detached and immobile camera position, and complex character relationships contributed to the film's inaccessibility for most audiences. What actually upsets some writers in the book is the "untrue" depiction of the February 28 Incident. They point to two specific scenes in the film that directly refer to the violence of the massacre; these scenes, however, show the Taiwanese mob's excessive hatred of the mainland Chinese rather than the Nationalist Party's machine-gun shooting of unarmed Taiwanese people.

These critics base their arguments on a conception of cinema that privileges a certain kind of legibility. If one slightly shifts one's attention from the search for the whole to the fragmentary, meanings unfold much more fluently. This shift in reading paradigm is evocatively described by Homi Bhabha's comparison in *Nation and Narration* between the "pedagogical" (the linear, sufficient, and complete master narrative), and the "performative" (the supplementary and temporal). Bhabha basically begins with many of Benedict Anderson's observations about the supposed antiquity and actual novelty of the nation, only Bhabha repackages them in poststructuralist clothing to provide both theoretical depth and a site for resistance. A typical characteristic of the nation is its propensity toward sinking roots to the depths of history, to stake a claim for its origin in a past that it simultaneously erases. In this process the nation creates a master narrative offered for the identification and participation of its people, who not only "belong" to it: they "constitute" and "perform" the nation.

In *City of Sadness* the pedagogical can be understood as the official story of the February 28 Incident. This is the specious official history that was sanctioned until recently. The performative indicates the representation of personal memory and individual experience against the political backdrop, diegetically presented in three discursive texts: sound, writing, and photography. As mentioned in our discussion of the controversy the film sparked, the multiple claims for legitimate authorship about the incident have created a polysemy in the reconstruction of Taiwan's history from 1945 to 1949. This knot of textual contention is particularly intense around the February 28 Incident. Therefore, these three discursive textualities provide an alternative approach to the history as well as an indirect, mediated, and trope-filled contestation with the official writing of the history of Taiwan.

Sound

Considering the historical neglect of sound in film criticism, it is not surprising that few critics have turned their attention to the crucial role played by the soundtrack in *City of Sadness.* First, the organization of the diegetic sound initiates the narrative and constitutes the nonvisual properties of the narrative. Second and more important, sound is organized by sexual difference and formulates the dialogism of the text. We can make this particularly evident through a comparison between feminine voice and masculine voice in relation to the narration of history and individual story. Before we engage the close analysis of specific sequences or shots, we must consider some of the theoretical models utilized in the analysis.

In *The Dialogical Imagination,* Mikhail Bakhtin defines the dialogical text as an "arena of conflict between two voices." In *The Dialogical Text,* Mary Ann Doane expands this concept to distinguish monological from dialogical texts in film. A monological text often conceals its voice in order to sustain the spectator's identification with the fiction, while a dialogical text manifests multiple voices to create multiple identifications. In a dialogical text, dispersed voice-over narration often disrupts the unisonic discoursing voice. In *The Acoustic Mirror,* Kaja Silverman suggests that in the classical Hollywood cinema, the soundtrack is organized by sexual difference. Male voice-over tends to be synchronized with visual track and associated with exteriority, that is, in the framing of the diegesis. Pointing to the fact that female nondiegetic narrators are virtually nonexistent in American feature films, Silverman argues that the male voice enjoys a privileged position in the text and is structured as the site of enunciation. Female voice-over, on the other hand, is temporally and spatially dislocated from the image track and associated with interior perspective. It is invariably confined by the diegesis, and so its position relative to the masculine voice is restricted from enunciative power.

Since *City of Sadness*'s female voice-over and female writing are closely linked in the diegesis, feminine voice and its relation with masculine voice in creating dialogic qualities will be discussed in the section on writing in a more cross-referenced analysis. The scope of this section applies primarily to the soundtrack itself. The diegetic sound in *City of Sadness* is organized in a polyvalent style and for the purposes of simplicity we divide our discussion into two sections in accordance with sexual difference: masculine voice and feminine voice.

Masculine Voice

In *The Acoustic Mirror* Kaja Silverman has suggested that female voice is aligned with interiority, confinement, and self-consciousness, while male voice-over is culturally and cinematically accepted as a synonym of direct, authoritative speech. The male voice is thus perceived as the source of knowledge and authority, as what Silverman designates as "the origin of the text." However, while it is true that the male voice is used to address historical facts, the manner in which it is placed in the context of the images creates a historical tension between the pedagogical and the personal. The male voices connected to the most powerful historical figures—the Japanese emperor, Chiang Kai-shek's governor Chen Yi 陳儀—are invisible rulers. The simultaneous visual absence and aural omnipresence of these powerful, patriarchal figures elicits a subtle, yet powerful, critique of colonial rule.

I. The Opening Scene

The radio broadcast of the Japanese emperor's speech announcing his nation's surrender provides the sonic landscape for the film's opening scene; the visual track depicts the birthing labor of the Oldest Brother's concubine. This first scene also provides the first example of a gendered diegetic voice that narrates the pedagogical speech of the nation. The soundtrack used here has an obvious historical referent as well as a metaphorical function. The sound of this famous speech signals the end of colonial rule in Taiwan along with Japanese imperial hegemony. The childbearing in return indicates the celebration of Taiwan's separation from Japan's colonial rule and a new era in the island's history. This moment was the first time people had heard the emperor's voice. As Japanese historian Tamura Tsuraeda points out, the transmission of the emperor's "pure" physical voice (at least for the local audience) reflects an indexical referent to a Japanese imperial sign of what she called *"yujin fangsong"* (presence of His Majesty's jade-like voice).

However, *yujin fangsong,* in the context of this period's history, holds complex connotations for Taiwanese listeners. When Taiwan became part of Japan's colonial territories at the beginning of the 20th century, the Taiwanese were forced to convert to the Japanese language and culture, what Anderson has called an "official nationalism" imposed from above. As a result, the fictional characters of the diegesis and those who experienced that process of colonization are afforded linguistic access to this speech, while most spectators are familiar with its sound but not its meaning (there are no subtitles for this sound). The opening diegetic sound thus serves as an indexical historical referent within both diegetic and extradiegetic levels.

II. Mandarin Lesson

The informative, authoritative male speech is also present in an early scene when the hospital staff is being trained to speak Mandarin to accommodate the influx of mainlanders. The shot (fig. 12) first shows Hinomi writing in her diary during a break, but her space is soon invaded by a male speaking voice. The next shot cuts into the space of an aged male teacher, who drills his students in Mandarin in a high-pitched, accented voice. Here the economy of shots efficiently articulates the scene's discursive dialogism by

Fig. 12. The arrival of the Nationalists is marked by a scene showing Hinomi writing in her diary, but her space is soon invaded by the sound of an aged male voice teaching nurses Mandarin in the next room.

juxtaposing private writing and pedagogical indoctrination. This simple class in Mandarin Chinese signifies not only a linguistic shift but also massive historical change: the arrival of the Nationalist regime and the abrupt replacement of Japanese culture by mainland Chinese culture.

III. The Prison Sequence

The sequence of Wen-ching in the prison depicts the Nationalist military's cold-blooded executions of Taiwanese (fig. 9). As in other parts of the film, the entire sequence is devoid of visual images of actual killing. Yet again, through the use of sound and verbal language, the terror is revealed. Here we focus only on the first half of the sequence. Constituted by only three long takes, the scene begins with the shot of a dim lamp on a wall with the diegetic sound of marching. The next shot cuts into a dark space where we can barely see a soldier's back as he leans forward to open a cell door. The door opens, and we hear the soldier bark, "Wu Chi-wen, Tsui Tung-ho, appear in court."

"Appearing in court," initially sounds like the prisoners are being summoned for their turn in the legal procession. However, the way the prisoners silently dress themselves, solemnly shake hands with their fellow prisoners, and the diegetic sounds of singing from other cells invoke the spectator's suspicion regarding what kind of court they are called to. As the prisoners walk out of the cell, and the door closes behind them, the long-take shot becomes dark and we hear that same marching sound. The scene finally cuts to the third shot where we see Wen-ching framed by the prison window. He looks offscreen, as though he could actually hear the fading footsteps of the guards and prisoners, but his face shows no reaction to the sharp report of rifles outside. For all but Wen-ching, the sounds of execution by gunfire punctuate the sonic orders of the guards (and their State), leaving a deadly silence in their wake.

Feminine Voice

The interior feminine voice is positioned at several points in the narrative to create irony that evokes a political awareness of the Nationalist brutality. The quiet ending of the film leaves us with a family deeply wounded by politics. With the emotional reactions restricted due to the imperatives of their patriarchal role, the range of the male characters' emotional reaction is limited. Thus, their frustration must be displaced onto illegitimate (underworld) institutions such as gambling, prostitution, and fighting. This is the only outlet for relief. Women, on the other hand, prove more capable of coping with the changes since they are excluded from the center of the political arena. However, their marginal position does not prevent them from being affected by the bloody political transition. Although most female characters in the film are deprived of a public speaking voice, their reaction to atrocity is still channeled through their "feminine" voice: usually hysterical screaming or weeping, gender codes kept strictly off-limits to Hou's male characters.

I. The Second Daughter-in-Law Cries

Hou never discloses the name of the wife of the third son, Wen-liang. She expresses her frustration and traumatic feelings on two occasions when her life is damaged by the ponderous, outside forces of history. The first one occurs when the military police rush into the house, attempting to arrest Wen-liang. It seems that a beating takes place in the offscreen spaces, but the wife's hysterical screaming and its sound communicates the brutality with more visceral power than any on-screen violence could muster. Another example comes with Wen-liang's homecoming after being released from

Fig. 13. A wife reads her husband's death note, scrawled in blood. Rather than rendering historical terror visually, Hou makes it perceptible through the sounds of women screaming.

prison. Upon arriving at the house, he passes out as a result of the cruelty he experienced during imprisonment. Seeing him in such a terrible state, the wife wails, calling his name in order to waken him. At the same time that she reacts hysterically to her husband's wounds, she expresses her deep shock, her emotional trauma.

II. "Father is innocent, you have to live with dignity."

Another example of the potential power of feminine voice occurs when Wen-ching, after being released from prison, visits the family of a friend who was secretly executed in prison. The victim's family was not able to receive his dead body, let alone conduct a proper funeral or hear the final words of their beloved family member. Thus Wen-ching must inform the wife and children of his death by delivering a message scrawled in the husband's own blood. The scene depicting Wen-ching's visit re-presents the private, unspoken sadness endured by countless families who were, and are, victims of the February 28 Incident.

This particular iteration of the sadness starts in a domestic setting, with Wen-ching sitting on the right side of the frame and three children standing in the middle, against an obscure backdrop. The dead man's wife enters the space, offering Wen-ching a cup of tea. Wen-ching then takes a tightly folded, strip-like cloth from a necktie. He unfolds the piece of the cloth and hands it to the woman. The unnamed, silent woman reads her husband's last words and loses control, bursting into tears. As we have argued, Hou reserves reverse angles for privileged moments. Here he cuts to the woman's point of view of the cloth. Scrawled in blood by finger are the words, "Father is innocent. You have to live with dignity." This melodramatic moment is not manifested by verbal language, but by gestures that depend on femininity as a means of expression. The terrors that have occurred out there in history have not been cinematically visualized. Rather, they have been made perceptible through the sound of women screaming. It is through women's gendered response to traumatic experiences that the film's figurative "sadness" is experienced by the spectator.

III. The Voice/Speech of Chen Yi (the Governor) vs. the Voice/Writing of Hinomi (the Housewife)

On the day after February 28, Governor Chen Yi's speech is broadcast across the nation's airwaves. The sequence begins with Chen Yi's soothing voice saying "Compatriots of Taiwan . . ." The speech continues into the next shot in the hospital office where the staff bends over the radio, concentrating on the broadcast. Chen Yi's speech denies the ferocity of the conflict, but in his benevolent tone he emphasizes the government's efficiency in consoling the victims. The scene then cuts to the hallway of the hospital where Hinomi meets her brother and Wen-ching. Although the soundtrack continues to carry the politician's broadcast, Hinomi's voice is soon superimposed over the governor's speech. Quoting from what she has heard from people's discussion, she writes "It is said that many people were killed in Taipei . . . everyone is afraid that one war is just over, how come another will soon begin?" Her writing is positioned to supersede and contradict Chen Yi's pedagogical statement.

Chen Yi's male speech is acoustically reinforced in presenting an exclusively authoritative mode. Without seeing his body, Chen Yi's authority is made "present" through his exterior, omnipresent speech. Through the device of radio, he and the State are aligned with the power of technology. The mise-en-scène is structured to indicate the infiltration of his verbal enunciation of the incident into the diegetic space of ordinary people. We see the hospital staff assembled around the radio from which his voice emanates; a doctor fiddles with a knob to clarify its transmission. However, by superimposing Hinomi's feminine, quiet, and private voice over his speech, a sonic irony emerges out of the friction of the two "grains" of voice, accompanied as well by two different versions of the incident. It is in the dialogical space formed by these tensions that an alternative, resistant reading of the history of the nation may be found. This dialogism finds its source in terms of the sexual difference in clarifying the two levels of voice. Therefore, to say that her diary is too private to be significant to politics is to repress her subjectivity, overlook a counternarrative of the nation, and lose the dialectical potential of performance of the people, replacing one pedagogy with another.

Writing

Many events that are not visualized in the film are represented through the traces of writing. Although the most important instances are Hinomi's diary and the intertitles for Wen-ching's communication with other characters, the film is full of examples. Hou Hsiao-hsien's ambition in articulating the origin of the narration of Taiwan is best exemplified in the intertitles, where writings carry the mythical and effective tropes in the genealogy of the nation. That this is accomplished through a character incapable of speech and hearing is one of the film's finer ironies.

Hinomi's writing is "heard" through her diegetic voice-over, which highlights femininity by forming a different voice for the history. It can be argued that women in Hou's films represent key signifiers for articulating domesticity and Oedipal anxiety. Hou's archetypical image of women has them cooking or folding clothes. Nevertheless, a question arises from this kind of scrutiny. Beyond the feminist cultural critique of women's subordination and marginality in Hou's filmic world, how may a spectator position her/himself at those moments of female narration in *A Time to Live and a Time to Die, Daughter of the Nile,* and most prominently, *City of Sadness,* where a woman's writing and her voice are positioned as the most important narrative agency throughout the entire film?

Dialogism and Feminine Voice

The article "Women Cannot Enter History?," written by Mi Zou in *The Death of the New Cinema,* centers around the negation of women in history and indicates the film's overall conservatism. Another article by Liao Ping-hui argues that the prominence of a feminine voice in the narration of the February 28 Incident betrays a similar "femininized" position towards the Nationalist government's brutality. Instead of manifesting a direct and persuasive voice in writing the history of the incident, the film's indirection is equivalent to the traditional definitions of femininity imposed by patriarchy—submissive, peaceful, and forgiving. Such qualities are reinscribed onto the position of the Taiwanese people in political movements, and immobilize dissent and oppositional readings of history.

Both arguments rightly decode the ideological masking provided by the phallocentric inscription of traditional femininity. However, their decoding rearticulates the very patriarchal mechanisms they painstakingly attempt to dissolve. Their arguments imply that the representation of traditional femininity can only be read as a result of patriarchal suppression rather than a possibility of resistance. This passive and "negative" assumption about femininity reinscribes phallocentric notions—that femininity can signify only by an anatomy of patriarchy—and obliterates the potential resistance embedded in the feminine voice and Hinomi's enunciation here. Certainly, one cannot deny the articulation of sexual difference as a fruitful approach in the examination of national and sexual politics. However, the emphasis on the monolithic reading of Hinomi's enunciation is to repress the expressive potential of women that may be read (or experienced) as positive, progressive resistance. Female voice, noise, and writing constitute the most crucial dialogism of the text.

I. The Introduction of Hinomi and Her Meeting with Wen-ching

Although *City of Sadness* is, in many ways, structured differently from classical Hollywood cinema, Silverman's model is useful for elaborating the dialogical text embodied by female voice. The film introduces Hinomi and Wen-ching through the voice-over of her diary when she describes her arrival at the hospital where she will work as a nurse. Her voice-over is synchronized with the image track in which we do see her carried by a bamboo chair, accompanied by Wen-ching, walking a mountain track. In this scene, her narration serves as a diegetic imperative; it is not characterized by confinement. Her voice-over is the mastering diegetic sound through which the whole scene is framed.

We can elaborate our argument further by considering Hinomi's writing more closely. Her narration serves as the site of enunciation for both private and public events, but these also represent two different kinds of textuality. The synchronization of female voice-over with its visual presentation only occurs when that narration has no indexical referent to the larger social context. These are scenes Hinomi directly experiences. However, when her voice-over describes public events, the visual presentation hardly synchronizes with the audio track. The image tracks in such cases are usually enunciated from a delayed quasi-omnipresent perspective that begins with Hinomi's act of writing/voice-over and then almost imperceptibly shifts to a presentation of her description with all the presence of omniscient cinematic narration. The third-person, godlike point of view retroactively justifies and legitimizes her fragmented and personal documentation of the history.

Given our comparison of the relationship between sound and image at the diegetic level, it is correct to see that Hinomi's narration of the public event is always taken over by the omniscient, macroenunciative voice. However, those synchronized scenes in which her subjectivity is privileged in the diegesis must still be seen as interdependent with the macroenunciative narration. Although her diary may appear trivial, private, and insignificant compared to the larger sociopolitical context, it is through reading along the borders of these two textualities that irony is produced and dialogic tension arises.

Pedagogical History and Personal Writing

I. Women's Time

In general dialogical textuality can be seen as a key mechanism in the various levels of writing. However, the question of how dialogism is produced through the contestation of female, personal memory and male, pedagogical history requires close attention. Julia Kristeva's influential essay "Woman's Time" is useful here in forming the distinction between the two discursive texts in relation to history. Kristeva identifies the time of history as linear time: time as project. It is characterized by an organic course organized by the tropes of departure, progress, and arrival. Feminine time in contrast is characterized as cyclical and monumental time, associated with repetition, reproduction, and eternity.

Kristeva's conception can be applied to two representations of history in *City of Sadness*. The masculine, patriarchal voice is coded through the rhetoric of grand speech and delivered in public spaces; the feminine voice, on the other hand, is written in diary form to sustain a desire to speak within a private space. The speech represented in the public sphere punctuates historical change and regulates discursive knowledge about history. The broadcast of the Japanese emperor's speech announcing the end of World War II in the film's opening sequence, the Mandarin lesson taught in the hospital, and the three instances of broadcast speeches made by Chen Yi serve the same function in the narrative. Moreover, the ordering of each pedagogical speech contains a consciously written periodization, forming the linear chronology of the nation's history from 1945 to 1949.

On the other hand, Hinomi's diary appears fragmented in relation to this version of history. As critic Li Shangren rightly says, in "Taiwanese New Cinema and Third World Cinema," Hinomi's time is never saturated into the linear course of the national historical project except for the times when she is narrating a man's story. Li's argument is based on one of the film's posters, which features an image of Wen-ching and Hinomi sitting on the futon with their baby when they receive a message informing them of Hinoe's fate. In the image, Wen-ching holds Hinomi in his arms and looks out into offscreen space, while Hinomi leans against him, looking down toward the futon, consumed with mourning for the loss of her brother. Li argues that Wen-ching's offscreen look indicates his association with the linear project of history, that is, worrying about the consequences of their relation with the anti-Nationalist compatriots. Hinomi, on the contrary, unable to respond to the cruel reality as immediately as her husband does, is primarily wracked by her feelings about the shocking news.

We argue that although her writing does not provide an overview of history, nor does it try to construct a total description of the political restructuring, it does however provide a micro version of the history written in the broadest of strokes. Besides telling men's stories, Hinomi's interference with the national history is also made perceptible by inserting her fragmentary writing into the diegesis. Here director Hou provides an aperture in the narrative space for the spectator to project his or her own readerly text, construed out of the traces of a woman's daily documentation of her life, which is written against the larger social and political forces.

II. Wen-ching Is Arrested

If we put the political incident aside and concentrate more on Hinomi's enunciation of the event, it is not difficult to find that the main part of her diary is all about her experience with the rituals of a woman's life in

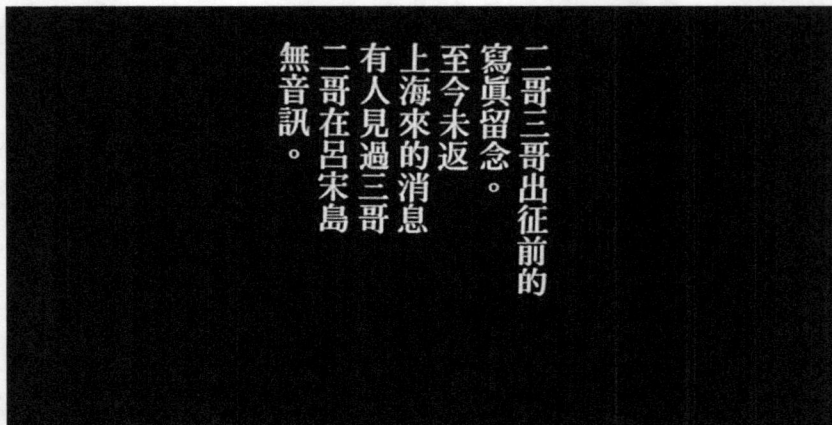

二哥三哥出征前的
寫眞留念。
至今未返
上海來的消息
有人見過三哥
二哥在呂宋島
無音訊。

Fig. 14. Wen-ching: "A photo before my brothers went to war. They have not returned since." As an unusual form of cinematic writing, the intertitles are obsessed with myth-telling and supplemental pedagogical history as another narration of the nation.

traditional society—romance, marriage, reproduction, nourishing, and the housewife's role in the daily life of the family. Her occupation of cyclical time is especially seen in the letter to her niece-in-law, where she writes about the arrest of Wen-ching. The letter ends with the description of seasonal change and beautiful scenery. Once again, the enclosure of a political incident in a natural, cyclic parameter can be conceived in an ironic tone. However, it is by injecting the personal into the political or vice versa that the representation of history and memory becomes more dynamic and complex. In this case, female subjectivity and feminine time represent an alternative mode of temporality at work throughout the history of civilization and hence, allows a powerful antithesis to contest the linear, hegemonic discourse of the nation's narration of its history.

Intertitles

It has been pointed out that the intertitles in the film are written in the Mandarin language, which cannot be verbalized in the Taiwanese dialects. This observation contradicts the historical reality that most Taiwanese did not speak Mandarin in the late 1940s. This seemingly accurate critique overlooks the entire body of the literary works written in Chinese by anticolonial Taiwanese novelists and poets during the occupation period. As literary scholar Lü Zhenghui suggests, anticolonial writers might not have been able to read aloud their writing in standard Mandarin; they wrote Chinese literature as an act of political resistance against colonialism. This helps explain why the writing in the intertitles appears quite "classical" compared to the verbal language of the Taiwanese. As the intertitles are presented in a form of writing, they are obsessed with myth-telling and supplemental pedagogical history as another narration of the nation.

I. "My brothers disappeared during the war."

The first intertitle in the film appears when Wen-ching first communicates with Hinomi through writing (fig. 14). Their conversation concerned a photo taken before Wen-ching's brothers went to war, forced to fight for the Japanese. The formal device for re-presenting the words of mute Wen-ching is modeled after a device of narrative agency from the silent cinema, where intertitles were utilized for narrative comprehension before the coming of recorded sound. The appropriation of this silent film device seems to have at least two important registers. One is obviously the diegetic: Wen-ching's inability to communicate through verbal language. The other important register is its aesthetic deployment. Why use intertitles, not subtitles?

The subtitle is the technology used at the close of the silent era to overcome the barriers between sonic linguistic frontiers. Conventionally, it sits at the edge of the screen, *translating* the dialogue in one language into another as discreetly and transparently as possible. In contrast, the intertitle of the silent era served double duty, to both give domestic actors voice and translate tongues. In *City of Sadness,* the silent film intertitle is used to convey nonverbal dialogue. As an aesthetic anachronism that present-day audiences are unaccustomed to, and as a nondiegetic, formal mechanism to transcribe the mute dialogue or stand in for an implied narrator, the intertitles of *City of Sadness* seem to generate their own presence. They resist subordination to the diegesis of the visual track. These graphic substitutions for the thoughts of characters stand in the interstices between visual representation and silence.

Putting the words against a black surface, the intertitle invites the spectator to "read" rather than to "see." Therefore, the contingent relationship between the visual track and the intertitle assures the latter's textual quality as writing. The next questions about the intertitles we must ask are, "What is the writing about? What is its relationship to the diegesis? What role does it play in the film's discourse about history, memory, and politics?" If we consider the tense of all the film's intertitles, it is not surprising to discover that relative to the temporal moment of the enunciation of the "speaker" (Wen-ching), they all involve the past, be it the recollection of personal history and public events or of folklore.

If we try to thematize or "totalize" the intertitles, we come to the conclusion that all of them are involved with the business of mythmaking. The writing of myth is particularly crucial in the allegorical construction of the nation's genealogy. As Benedict Anderson suggests, cultural specificity has been the exclusive domain of the nation as it constructs the identity of its national culture. Similarly, part of Hou's ambition in *City of Sadness* extends beyond the mere representation of a political incident from the distant past. In addition to the trope of birth, or rebirth, of the nation as embodied in the opening sequence, the project of narrating the nation also requires the inclusion of the "past," or to be exact, the "origin" of the nation. It seems that there is no better way to narrate the origin of a nation without first setting up its geographic specificity. Perhaps this can explain why the first intertitle of the film concerns the whereabouts of Wen-ching's second brother (went missing in the Philippines) and his third brother (who is said to have been seen in Shanghai). The geographic mapping of the locations of the brothers ranges from the Philippines to the Chinese mainland. This mapping seems to imply the linkage of Taiwan with her neighboring islands in the Pacific and, more significantly, with mainland China, which has been serving as the defining geographical matrix for Han Chinese living in Taiwan. By sketching a geographic map of the Lin family's missing sons, the physical locale of Taiwan is subtly and successfully oriented.

II. Hinomi and Wen-ching in Their Private World

Perhaps the most evident mythmaking for creating the genealogy of nation can be drawn from the intimate communication between Wen-ching and Hinomi. This scene (fig. 15) begins with a discussion of politics and social problems during a social gathering at Wen-ching's house. While the political discussion continues at the center of the room, Wen-ching and Hinomi soon move to their private world, communicating with each other through music and writing. First, Wen-ching plays a record of "Lorelei," a famous German song, and Hinomi writes to him about the story of the song. The story tells about a beautiful siren whose charms become fatal attractions to

Fig. 15. Wen-ching and Hinomi soon move to their private world, communicating with each other through music and writing.

many enchanted sailors. The insertion of a German folk myth seems anachronistic. Yet, it helps situate a presymbolic stage before the totality of a national concept comes into being.

III. Wen-ching's Childhood

The mythical aura also exists in Wen-ching's writing of his own story, in which he talks about his childhood desire to become a cross-dressing opera actor. The image track then visualizes his writing, bringing us back to a mythical past first by presenting a costumed actor performing in a rural location where villagers gather around in an outdoor space, watching opera. Then the shot cuts to a group of nearby children mimicking the actor. Before the visualization of the writing about a childhood story, Wen-ching has mentioned how his wish was ridiculed by his teacher because opera was regarded as a trade comparable to prostitution. The male performer's role in opera was especially controversial because women were excluded from the trade, leaving all female roles to male actors. Given the gender ambiguity in opera, the male performer's sexual appeal was often exposed to homophobic ridicule. Bearing this history in mind, Wen-ching's memory of his child-hood before he lost his hearing suggests the presymbolic, precolonial Taiwan dominated by a mythical aura and infused with the spectacle of traditional opera, gender ambiguity, and innocence.

The mythical past embodied in the intertitles continues in the sequence where Hinoe and Hinomi tell Wen-ching about a popular Meiji era story of a young woman who killed herself before she could be stricken by age and disease. This story, as Wen-ching was told, kindled the collective passion of Japanese youth during the Meiji restoration period. It introduces Wen-ching to a tale of sacrifice for the prosperity of the modern nation; this may serve as a pedagogical cue, and later prompts a choice to sacrifice his life for the sake of Taiwan, as it transforms from a colony to a country.

Photography

> The Photograph does not call up the past. . . . The effect it pro-duces upon me is not to restore what has been abolished (by time, by distance) but to arrest that what I see has indeed existed.
>
> —Roland Barthes, *Camera Lucida*

In *City of Sadness,* the photograph is a nonverbal access point to both his-tory and memory. Critics attacked the construction of the film's main char-acter, Wen-ching, who is deaf and cannot speak, as a passive, handicapped photographer who cannot actively react against the ruling power. By way of contrast, minor characters offer far more powerful models of resistance, such as Hinomi's brother, Hinoe, who escapes to the mountains and organizes a socialist commune after the massacre. If we are to take Hou's explanation for this character at face value, we would recognize a simple, practical reason for Wen-ching's handicaps: the Hong Kong actor selected to play the role, Tony Leung Chiu-wai, could speak neither Mandarin nor Taiwanese Amoy fluently; muteness solves the problem. Yet, sometimes such technical eclecti-cism generates more interesting and provocative results. Since Wen-ching loses the primary faculty of speech for articulating his relationship with his-tory he must rely on other means of communication, such as his photog-raphy. Still photography becomes an alternative mode of representation for history and memory.

It is through his photographic images that history is written and memory is recollected. Photography becomes a mediated arresting of the past. By superimposing individual experience against the political context, photography becomes not only a sign granting access to the past but also a comment on history. Thus, the photos' relationship with history is highly coded. Each photo signifies different phases of historical development embodied by a double play of arrival and departure, both literally and metaphorically. The following close analysis of three photographs will demonstrate this codification of temporality.

Photograph 1: The Reopening of the "Little Shanghai" (a
Japanese-Style Teahouse)—Rebirth and Restoration

Following the first sequence of Japan's surrender and the birth of Older Brother's son, the second sequence begins with the diegetic sound of fire.

Fig. 16. A Japanese-speaking photographer shoots a photograph of the staff at the grand opening of the Little Shanghai restaurant.

The festive mode announced in the beginning continues to dominate the whole sequence. This is the preparation and celebration for the reopening of businesses that were prohibited by the Japanese administration. The motif of rebirth and restoration is obvious, given the simultaneous occurrence of the biological birth of an individual and the historical rebirth of a nation binding each other in the preceding sequence. At the end of the scene, the entire family (except Wen-ching and the missing brothers) gathers in front of the teahouse to have their photograph taken. After the photographer snaps the shutter, the photographic event itself becomes a snapshot still image, reinforcing the historical and cultural meaning of the celebration of the rebirth and restoration of the nation.

Photograph 2: The Japanese Teacher and His Girl
Students—Deportation of the Japanese after World War II

The liberation from Japanese colonialism means the departure of the Japanese residents from their ex-colony. In this scene, we see Wen-ching at work

Fig. 17. Wen-ching photographs a departing Japanese teacher and his Taiwanese students; his photograph encapsulates the ambiguous relationship between the colonizer and the colonized. Note eyelines.

as a professional photographer for the first time. The subjects in his studio include a group of Taiwanese junior high school girls and their Japanese teacher. This photographic event has a historical referent. It indicates an early stage of the transitional period from 1945 to 1949 when the Japanese residents in Taiwan were ordered to leave. In addition to its historical reference, this photo encapsulates the ambiguous relationship between the colonizer and the colonized. It implies that to some extent, during the fifty years of occupation, the Japanese also built up genuine relationships with Taiwanese beyond the master/slave prototype of colonialism. As a result, the simple vision of looking at all Japanese as exploitative colonizers is problematic. The photo paves the way for the narrative development of the next several scenes in which this ambivalent relationship is illustrated. The latter part of the sequence reveals the emotional bond between Wen-ching, Hinoe, and their Japanese teacher. This interethnic relation is also shown in the friendship between Hinomi and her Japanese friend, the daughter of their teacher. The end of colonialism breaks these intimate relationships.

Photograph 3: The Last Picture of Wen-ching, Hinomi, and Their Son—A Signifying Process of Double Meaning, of Preservation and Destruction

Perhaps the most devastating moment in the film is when Wen-ching takes a photograph of his family when realizing that his own death is near. Their

Fig. 18. Wen-ching takes a photograph of his family when he realizes that his own death is near. Note eyelines.

constrained pose and worried looks, emphasized by a frozen cinematic image that doubles the diegetic still photo, constitute the most revealing performative representation undermining any pedagogical interpretation of history. From the first shot of the scene (the ritual preparation for photo taking—combing his hair, setting up the camera, adjusting the lens and shutter) to the last freeze-frame shot of the family photo, the scene reveals an appalling message about how this single family is damaged by political brutality. This image constitutes the most powerful accusation against the pedagogical history written by the Nationalist regime for the way it teases out the double meaning of the coexistence of presence and absence in the photographic image.

The subsequent voice-over by Hinomi foregrounds this double-coding. With a freeze-frame coinciding with the click of the shutter, the filmic frame collides with the photographic frame. The frozen image disperses into the results of two apparatuses. Finally, the film pauses on the "doubled" image for several seconds, waiting for Hinomi's sound to provide a sequential transition. Hinomi's voice-over informs us of the final event following that photo session—the arrest of her husband. Linking the photographic and filmic image of the family, Wen-ching's last effort to keep his nuclear family intact through the means of a still photograph thus makes a powerful image, an allegory and a lament for a nation eroded by colonial forces. Given this highly charged photographic signification of destruction and preservation, the role of the deaf photographer, who is unable to speak, can no longer be understood as a technical compromise but rather a highly selective choice that invests more compelling, emotive meanings in filmic images.

4 / Distant Analysis/Close Analysis

A double-movement between near and far. The closer the critic approaches, the more distanced the object seems to become. Can analysis suggest how the bits and pieces of its violent work move in concert? Perhaps we need to move away to see closer. As we near the conclusion of this book, we turn from a close analysis that dismantles the film into small pieces to a "distant analysis."

This chapter gathers our scattered musings, which jumped across the breadth of the film, to examine a single sequence from *City of Sadness*. It is an attempt to chart all the issues raised in our close analysis, but following Hou Hsiao-hsien's lead and carefully moving from one shot to the next. In this sequence—or sequence of sequence shots—we see the family through the death of the Oldest Son, his funeral, the marriage of Wen-ching (Youngest Son) and Hinomi, the birth of their son, and finally the death of Hinomi's brother. This manifold narrative movement (in only fifteen minutes of screen time) provides opportunities to discuss all the elements central to *City of Sadness,* from the obvious use of long takes to the subtle difference of his representation of violence, the writing of history, and the narration of the nation. All this takes place in seventeen shots, the unit by which we have segmented the analysis.

1—A [Shanghainese] smuggler and his men walk down the hallway of a bar, and an offscreen knife fight involving the Oldest Brother bursts into the background. The smuggler shoots Oldest Brother, who drops to the floor and dies with a shudder (a single shot, 38 seconds in length).

Any segmentation is ultimately arbitrary, and important connections naturally bleed from the preceding and subsequent scenes. This is the last shot of a long sequence filled with unpredictable cuts. It begins with a card game with the Oldest Brother, moves to a bathroom where his brother-in-law trades verbal jabs with one of the Shanghainese smugglers. Their insults escalate into a deadly encounter, which starts when the brother-in-law lunges from offscreen space with a knife. This starts a sequence that demonstrates Hou's propensity to secret away potential violence into offscreen space. The knife fight surges between on- and offscreen space in subsequent shots, from the bathroom to the hallway to the Oldest Brother's card game. At the beginning of this segment's shot, the rival boss leads his wounded soldier down this familiar hallway, when once again the sounds of struggle come in from unseen places. Oldest Brother jumps into the hallway and on-screen space, followed by two knife-wielding gangsters. Blades flash and bodies jerk to a violent dance, barely contained by the static frame of the screen until yet another unexpected element—a gunshot—both escalates and stops the violence.

2—A solitary bird floats above dark, misty mountains (22 seconds).
The hot yellow tones of the hallway give way to a chilling mist that obscures all but a trace of distant mountain ridges. It is an utterly empty transitional space filled up with diffused tension. A solitary crow cuts lazy arcs through the clouds, forecasting death. Funeral music fades in over the sound of wind.

3—The family huddles under umbrellas during Oldest Brother's funeral. A man walks to one side and picks up one of the ceremony's props . . . (32 seconds).

4—. . . and begins burning it in a pyre next to the onlookers. The funeral music begins to fade (49 seconds).
The family stands, motionless, enveloped by fog, holding an image of Oldest Brother. This is as close to the family as Hou will bring us; it is as close as we need to be, for it is not an individual tragedy. It's the sadness of a family, a community, a country. This is why the second shot—taken from the same camera axis only further removed—is far from redundant. Its recession is also an expansion; the further the camera moves the more mourners it includes.

5—On an expansive mountain overlooking the ocean, a wedding procession appears in the far distance (37 seconds).

As if completing the camera's retreat from the previous shot and book-ending it with another shot of the landscape, we see an expansive view of mountains and ocean on a fair, sunny day. Initially a space in which to pause and reflect on the passing of Oldest Brother, it abruptly shifts to a new beginning. Gradually, the sounds of music slowly fade in and the tiny figures of a procession crawl across a distant hill. At some point, we register this as wedding music and suddenly grasp an indeterminate ellipsis that occurred with the previous cut. An ending gives way to a new beginning, perhaps suggesting the beginning of a cycle, or the middle of a cycle if one reaches back to the opening scene of the film.

6—The family enters its home, filling a room dominated by the family shrine. Wen-ching and Hinomi begin their wedding by praying to their ancestors (31 seconds).

Latticed windows of a sliding door separate the camera from the shrine room, fracturing the frame into a myriad of quadrilaterals. In the midst of this bewildering, geometric space, surrounded by relatives both living and dead, Hinomi and Wen-ching take their vows. (See shots 6 through 9 in fig. 7.)

7—Facing the camera, the couple bow before the family shrine (28 seconds).

In what appears to be a continuous cut to a perfectly executed reverse-shot, the couple receives incense. They bow to show their respect to family members who have come before them. The focus of attention, they are also perfectly centered in the frame—though each bow leaves the family in the background watching.

8—The couple continue their bows with the patriarch and his daughter-in-law looking on (27 seconds).

A reverse-shot complementing the previous reverse-shot, this ignores the "common sense" of camera placement in favor of the logic of Hou and the law of the family. Hinomi and Wen-ching are no longer centered, but have been moved to the periphery, the left edge of the frame. This brings Old Man Lin to our attention; as Hinomi continues her bows, he observes approvingly. Decentering the couple brings to the fore the dynamic of the bride's entry into the Lin family sphere, a territory intimately linked to the cinematic space of the house. This shot aligns its view with the axis initiated early in the film and invoked again by the first shot of the wedding scene . . .

9—The couple bow to each other, and the ceremony ends with applause (38 seconds).

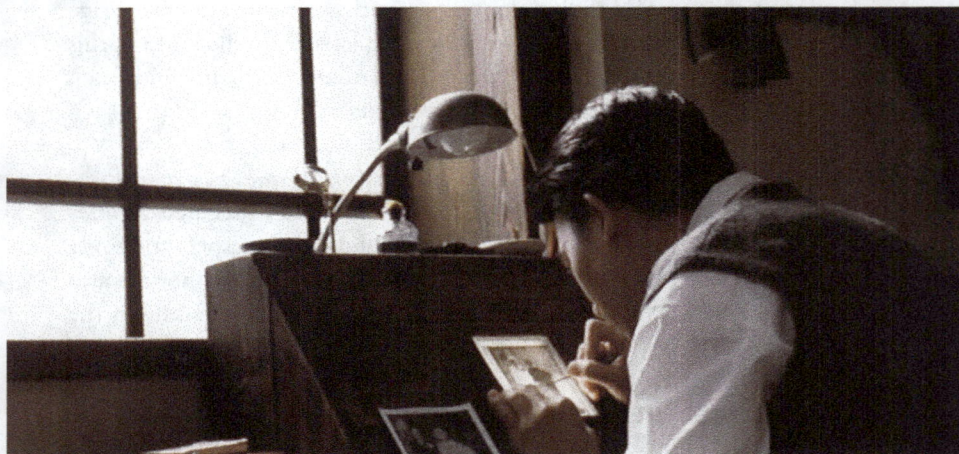

Fig. 19. In a quiet economy of restraint, Hou marks and divides the social space of the couple. Hinomi collects food, bears children; Wen-ching works, provides. Within only two shots, we are graphically presented the gender divisions of the nuclear family.

. . . and repeated once again in the last shot of the wedding. The camera pulls back on the axis, moves through the glass doors, and returns to the original camera placement. The ceremony ends with a view of the family, competing with the graphic force of the windows and doors of the room.

10—Outside, people mill around a market street below a jumble of roofs slanted this way and that. Soon Hinomi wanders out of the background and slowly makes her way to the foreground to buy vegetables. It soon becomes evident that she is with child (1 minute, 8 seconds).

Beginning as a transition emphasizing the graphic qualities of the jumbled buildings and the milling market they contain, this shot also marks a typically undecidable ellipsis. The amount of time elapsed since the wedding is hidden until the figure of Hinomi removes herself from the crowd. She approaches the camera, drawing our attention away from the play of the rooftops and toward the unmistakable dress and gait of impending motherhood.

11—At his light table, Wen-ching touches up his wedding photo (37 seconds).

Gently touching brush to negative, Wen-ching perfects the representation of his own wedding, his new stage in life. In a quiet economy of restraint, Hou marks and divides the social space of the couple. Hinomi collects food, bears children; Wen-ching works, provides. Within only two shots, we are graphically presented the gender divisions of the nuclear family.

12—Still very pregnant, Hinomi carefully sits down at the dinner table and places food in her mute husband's bowl. She takes away the book he reads, and they eat together, silently (1 minute, 45 seconds).

Scenes of eating acquire ritual significance in the films of Hou Hsiao-hsien. However, the offering at this meal departs from the standard fare. The Lin family table seats men only, but here in the nuclear family individual interaction has value. Wen-ching's intense concentration on his reading displaces the usual gendered hierarchy (the table reserved for patriarchs). Categories shift, though no verbal communication is possible. Silent communion is better than the distractions of the page.

13—Wen-ching leads Hinomi through the entrance of the hospital, while thunder rumbles in the background (39 seconds; fig. 8, lower right).

Hinomi and Wen-ching walk into another geometric space. Like the shots of the rooftops and the wall of windows, this view of the hospital entrance also emphasizes the bold graphic shapes marking the composition. The entrance is a graceful, white archway that gleams in the sunlight. In the background outside, a set of stairs stand at an angle, playing off the semicircle of the entranceway. This has previously framed the victims of massacre; now the camera has retreated so far back on its axis that a second, dark door acts as the gateway for a new life in the world . . . but thunder rolls in the distance, and the camera sits in darkness.

14—Rain falls quietly over the distant bay (25 seconds).

The interior, cyclical, eternal property of woman's time. Writing, we explore within our private self. Writing. Hinomi voices her thoughts on the damp weather. In a knot of intertwining sound and image, Hinomi's diary, the sound of her voice, the rolling thunder and drizzling rain condense, punctuating the moment with her subjectivity. Sound/writing/image work in concert to reassure and affirm her private and self-sustaining world.

15—Hinomi writes in her diary; her year-old baby skirts around the table, playing (2 minutes, 29 seconds).

The diary wanders. One place to another place. Nature, brother, baby, family, failing economy, declining supplies—all disseminate through her voice. Fragmentary, temporal descriptions of her private life and social, public situation supplement and document the intrusion of history into the personal. Hinomi's diary writes the history of the nation. The quiet interiority of the feminine voice. The temporal privacy of female writing. Both register a supplementary history through writing. Insignificant in the face of massive social and political change? Perhaps. But certainly the diary dwells in history understood as representation inscribed by countless discursive forces.

16—At night, a stranger knocks on the door, and hands a letter to Wen-ching (45 seconds).

A message arrives in the dark; by now it is no secret that writing often brings ominous tidings.

17—Hinomi feeds their baby on their futon. Wen-ching sits down, gives her the note, and they cry in each other's arms (2 minutes, 24 seconds).

The written word often communicates the most central events in this *City of Sadness;* though we are not privy to the contents of this letter, we know from their silent devastation that it announces the death of Hinomi's brother. The scene takes place in the same place, repeated in the same view, as when they first met. Oblivious to their grief, the baby plays around them as the sound of struggle fades in from unknown spaces. Although this shot approaches three minutes in length, most shots in this sequence are near the film's average of forty-two seconds. They mark a patient, regular rhythm, and all but three are perfectly still. These images contain scant narrative action . . . the spaces between them are an entirely different matter. Not only has time passed in enormous temporal gaps, but the narrative has moved in corresponding leaps: from death to funeral to wedding to pregnancy to birth to childhood and tragically back to death. Long takes play off their

Fig. 20. The written word often communicates the most central events in *City of Sadness*; though we are not privy to the contents of this letter, we know from their silent devastation that it announces the death of Hinomi's brother.

ellipses, creating a dialectic between narrative stasis and drastic movement. A temporal contrast between real and elided time, both brought under an overarching cyclical structure connected to the revolution of life and death. The final cut marking the end of this sequence initiates a flashback to the brother's capture by KMT troops, structurally mimicking the turning-back motion of the larger life cycle.

Conclusion

> [T]here is what may be called a criticism-led approach to national cinema, which tends to reduce national cinema to the terms of a quality art cinema, a culturally worthy cinema steeped in the high-cultural and/or modernist heritage of a particular national state, rather than one which appeals to the desires and fantasies of the popular audiences.
>
> —Andrew Higson, "The Concept of National Cinema"

> [T]he temporal dimension in the inscription of these political entities . . . serves to displace the historicism that has dominated discussions of the nation as a cultural force. The focus on temporality resists the transparent linear equivalence of event and idea that historicism proposes.
>
> —Homi Bhabha, "DissemiNation"

It seems strategically unwise and awkward to cite these two quotes to conclude our project on *City of Sadness*. Higson's reconceptualization of national cinema is in debt to the idea proposed by Thomas Elsaesser in his work on New German Cinema, in which he suggests that we should acknowledge that popular culture is an important and legitimate narrative form of national life. This leads us to rethink *City of Sadness* in the context of Taiwan and Taiwanese cinema, given the fact that the film has been criticized by the domestic audience for its high art style of representation.

We, however, do not intend to engage the high art/low culture debate here. Rather, we think that although popular cinema is a crucial register in discussing national cinema in more general terms, it is also important not to exclude important films that creatively deal with the complex concept of nation, and which are intent on exploring the specificity of the film medium.

It is true that we emphasize the aesthetics of Hou Hsiao-hsien's filmmaking and how his style mediates the representation of politics, even to the extent of alienating many in the audience. However, we suggest that the discontent expressed by the audience and the political critics precisely reveals the problematics of filmic totality. So what drove the Taiwanese to fill theaters for *City of Sadness*? Hou's film even outgrossed the simultaneously released *Miracles—Mr. Canton and Lady Rose* (Qi ji 奇蹟), Jackie Chan's major 1989 production. It is likely that the Taiwanese craving for images and narrations of the February 28 Incident contributed to Hou's commercial triumph over Golden Harvest's major action-adventure film, the first time that a New Cinema filmmaker ever outperformed the kung fu megastar, Jackie Chan. But it is the denial of that desire—the scopophilia of massacre—that upsets viewers.

Hou's thoughtful restraint in representing violence seems to indicate his ambivalence to the filmic image. Yet, it is this ambivalence that lends the narration of Taiwan dynamic complexity. Here it is helpful to return to Homi Bhabha's comments in the second epigraph. Bhabha uses deconstructionist vocabulary such as temporality to expand the concept of nation in order to include diasporic narration, subaltern writing, minority discourse, and any articulation based upon deconstructionist rhetoric. While perhaps Hou is not historically correct in depicting Taiwan's society—as has been pointed out by many historians—and his disjunctive form of representation arguably discredits his politics, the film provides an excellent stage to discuss a nation that has historically developed a culture of hybridity, a state of multiple, colliding ethnicities and languages.

Had Hou provided those dissatisfied spectators direct images of the massacre in a style purged of ambiguity—the manner in which a popular film would treat this history—his film would likely have held none of its power. Hou probably would have produced a film analogous to the frightening clarity of the Nationalist Party, replacing one pedagogical monologism with another. However, by staging the traumatic memories of the nation through its charged spaces and double writing, the film re-presents history with all its uncertain multiplicities. Whether it enlightened its audience will be endlessly debated and is ultimately inconsequential. The film finally helped bring the February 28 Incident into public discourse and sparked discussions about the character of the nation precisely through its multiple entry points. The health of a nation—and a national cinema—depends upon being open to this complexity.

Bibliography

City of Sadness Credits

A City of Sadness (Beiqing chengshi)

Taiwan, 1989
Director: Hou Hsiao-hsien (Hou Xiaoxian)
Distributor: Artificial Eye. Production Company: 3-H Films. An Era International
  Presentation. Executive Producers: H. T. Jan, Michael Yang. Producer: Qiu
  Fusheng. Associate Producer: Huakun. Production Managers: Tuo Zongmin,
  He Jingping, Xu Sixian, Wu Zhongliang.

Production Crew

Assistant Directors: Huang Jianhe, George Chang. Screenplay: Wu Nianzhen, Zhu
  Tianwen. Photographer: Chen Huai'en. Assistant Photographers: Liu Chang-
  hou, Zhao Faquan, Zhang Dalong, Wang Yunming. Intertitle Photography:
  Liu Deguang. Lighting: Song Diansheng. Editor: Liao Qingsong. Production
  Designers: Liu Zhihua, Lin Chongwen. Music: Tachikawa Naoki, Zhang Hon-
  gzyi. Music Performed by: Sens. Music Produced by: Cai Zhen'nan, Funhouse
  Inc. Wedding Music performed by: Yiwanran Zhangzong Groups. "Exile Tril-
  ogy" Music: Chen Jianzhong, Shang Yu, Lai Xihuang. Costumes: Zhu Jingwen.
  Sound Recording: Du Duzhi, Yang Jing'an. Production Assistants: Wan Guoxi-
  ang, Ding Shaobai. Ruantan Opera sequence staged by: Pan Yujiao. Subtitles:
  Stan Lai, Shu Kei.

Cast

Li Tianlu (Lin Ah-Lu), Chen Songyong (Lin Wen-Hsiung), Gao Jie (Lin Wen-Liang), Tony Leung (Lin Wen-Ching), Wu Yifang (Wu Hinoe), Xin Shufen (Wu Hinomi), Chen Shufang (Mio, First Brother's Wife) Ke Suyun (Second Brother's Wife), Lin Liqing (Third Brother's Wife), He Aiyun (First Brother's Mistress), Kenny Cheung (Ah Ga), Yang Changjiang (Ah Ga's Father), Ling Yang (Mr. Ko), Liu Yiubin (Man from Wenzhou), Huang Qianru (Ah Shueh), Luo Chengye (Ah Kun), Nakamura Ikuyo (Ogawa Shizuko), Nagatani Sentaro (Ogawa), Lin Zhaoxiong (Ah Cheng), Lin Ju (Kim Tsua), Zhang Wenzhong (Kim Chuan), Lu Qing (Mr. Wu), Mei Fang (Mrs. Wu), Lei Ming (Man from Shanghai), Wen Shuai (Ah Soa), Bi Li (Billy), Lai Denan (Hospital Administrator), Li Jianbin and Ye Zhizhong (Doctors), Ai Zaitu ("Red Monkey"), Chen Yurong (Ah Tsun), A Pipe (Ah Kio), Ye Wutong (Stallholder), Liu Zhuolun (Photographer), Xiao Chengji, Xhao Zhiyuan, and Zhang Fangcheng (Bodyguards), Yan Chun-chun (Nurse), Takakuwa Junko (Japanese Woman), Ma Wenhou (Ruantan Opera Actress), H. T. Jan (Mr. Lin), Wu Nianzhen (Mr. Wu), Xie Caijun (Mr. Xie), Zhang Dachun (Mr. He), Jin Shijie (Mr. Huang), Gao Chongli (Heavy), Chen Liangyue (Army Officer).

14,464 ft. 160 mins. Mandarin, Hokkien, Shanghaiese, Cantonese, and Japanese dialogue.

IMDB link: http://www.imdb.com/title/tt0096908.

Select Bibliography

It has been over two decades since the project made its debut and since then many new works on the film, Hou Hsiao-hsien, and Taiwanese cinema have been published. The list below is a partial update to the growing field of Taiwanese cinema and not to be taken as a definitive record.

Anderson, Benedict. *Imagined Communities: Reflections on the Origin and Spread of Nationalism* (London: Verso, 1983).

Bakhtin, Mikhail. *The Dialogical Imagination* (Austin: University of Texas Press, 1981).

Bakhtin, Mikhail. *Problems of Dostoevsky's Poetics.* Trans. R. W. Rotsel (Ann Arbor, MI: Ardis Press, 1973).

Barthes, Roland. *Camera Lucida.* Trans. Richard Howard (New York: Hill and Wang, 1981).

Berry, Chris, ed. "China's New 'Women's Cinema.'" *Camera Obscura* 18 (1988): 8–19.

Berry, Chris. *Perspectives on Chinese Cinema* (Bloomington: Indiana University Press, 1992).

Berry, Michael. "Words and Images: A Conversation with Hou Hsiao-hsien and Chu Tien-wen." *Positions—East Asia Cultures Critiques* 11.3 (2003): 675–716. Also in *Speaking in Images: Interviews with Contemporary Chinese Filmmakers,* ed. Michael Berry, 234–71 (New York: Columbia University Press, 2005).

Bhabha, Homi J. *Nation and Narration* (New York: Routledge University Press, 1990).

Bordwell, David. "Hou, or Constraints." In *Figures Traced in Light: On Cinematic Staging*, 186–237 (Berkeley: University of California Press, 2005).

Bordwell, David. *Ozu and the Poetics of Cinema* (Princeton: Princeton University Press, 1988); electronic version (Ann Arbor: University of Michigan Center for Japanese Studies, 2007), https://www.cjspubs.lsa.umich.edu/electronic/faculty series/list/series/ozu.php.

Bordwell, David. "Watch Again! Look Well! Look! (For Ozu)." *Observations on Film Art* (12 December 2013). http://www.davidbordwell.net/blog/2013/12/12/ watch-again-look-well-look-for-ozu/.

Brown, Georgia. "Island in the Mainstream." *Village Voice* (26 April 1989): 66.

Browne, Nick. "Hou Hsiao Hsien's *The Puppetmaster:* The Poetics of Landscape." In *Island on the Edge: Taiwan New Cinema and After,* ed. Chris Berry and Feii Lu, 79–88 (Hong Kong: Hong Kong University Press, 2005).

Burnett, Colin. "Parametric Narration and Optical Transition Devices: Hou Hsiao-hsien and Robert Bresson in Comparison." *Senses of Cinema* 33 (2004). http://sensesofcinema.com/2004/feature-articles/hou_hsiao_hsien_bresson/.

Burton, Julianne. "Marginal Cinemas and Mainstream Critical Theory." *Screen* 13.3 (1985): 3–21.

Canby, Vincent. "Why Some Movies Don't Travel Well." *New York Times* (23 October 1988): E1.

Chai, Lingling. "Dianying, lishi rentong yu renming jiyi" [Cinema, historical identification and popular memory], *Zili Zaobao* [Independent Morning Post] (27 December 1989): 14.

Chang, Jinn-pei. *Ning wang shi dai: chuanyue Beiqing chengshi ershi nian* [Looking Back through the film *A City of Sadness*] (Taipei: Tianyuan chengshi, 2011).

Chen, Fangming. *Er'er'ba shijian xueshu lunwenji* [Collected research works on the February 28 Incident] (Taipei: Qianwei, 1989).

Chen, Kuan-hsing, Paul Willemen, and Ti Wei, eds. "Hou Hsiao-hsien Special Issue." *Inter-Asia Cultural Studies* 9.2 (June 2008).

Chen, Qinan. *Jiazhu yu shehuei* [Clan and society] (Taipei: Linking, 1990).

Chen, Yenyu. *The February 28 Incident: Collected Works by Concerned Scholars* (Taipei: Council on Formosan Studies, 1992).

Cheng, Jihua, Li Shaobai, and Xing Zuwen. *Zhongguo dianying fazhanshi* [A history of the development of Chinese cinema], 2 vols. (Beijing: China Film Press, 1980).

Chi, Robert. "Getting It on Film: Representing and Understanding History in *A City of Sadness*." *Tamkang Review* 29.4 (Summer 1999): 47–84.

Chiao, Hsiung-ping. "Cinema: Autobiographical Masterpiece." *Free China Review* 38.2 (February 1988): 33–35.

Chiao, Hsiung-ping. "Cinema: Contrasting Images." *Free China Review* 38.2 (February 1988): 12–19.

Chiao, Hsiung-ping. "Cinema: Satire with Elegant Sensitivity." *Free China Review* 38.2 (February 1988): 36–39.

Chiao, Hsiung-ping. "Cinema: Struggles between Commercialism and Art." *Free China Review* 38.2 (February 1988): 20–25.

Chiao, Hsiung-ping. "*A Summer at Grandpa's*—Fields/Days of Infancy/Parent-Child Relationships." *Wave* (Tokyo) 21 (January 1989): 84–86.

Chiao, Hsiung-ping. *Taiwan xindianying* [The Taiwan New Cinema] (Taipei: Shibao, 1988).

Chiao, Hsiung-ping. *Xianggang dianying fengmao* [Features of Hong Kong Cinema] (Taipei: Shibao, 1987).

Chow, Rey. "Silent Is the Ancient Plain: Music, Filmmaking, and the Conception of Reform in China's New Cinema." *Discourse* 12.2 (1990): 82–90.

Chow, Rey. *Women and Chinese Modernity* (Minneapolis: University of Minnesota Press, 1990).

Chua, Lawrence. "Who's Hou?" *Women's Wear Daily* (7 September 1989).

Clark, Paul. *Chinese Cinema: Culture and Politics since 1949* (Cambridge: Cambridge University Press, 1987).

Clifford, James. *The Predicament of Culture: Twentieth-Century Ethnography, Literature, and Art* (Cambridge: Harvard University Press, 1988).

Cooke, David. "A Review of Hou Hsiao-hsien's *A City of Sadness*." *Public Culture* 5 (1993): 354–57.

Daly, Fergus. "On Four Prosaic Formulas Which Might Summarize Hou's Poetics." *Senses of Cinema* 12 (2001). http://sensesofcinema.com/2001/12/hou/#filmo.

Davis, Darrell William. "Borrowing Postcolonial: Wu Nien-chen's *Dou-san* and the Memory Mine." *Post Script* 20.2–3 (Winter–Spring 2001): 94–114. Also in *Chinese-Language Film: Historiography, Poetics, Politics,* ed. Sheldon H. Lu and Emilie Yueh-yu Yeh, chap. 11 (Honolulu: University of Hawaii Press, 2005).

Davis, Darrell William. "A New Taiwan Person? Questions for Wu Nien-chen." *positions: east asia cultures critique* 11.3 (Winter 2003): 717–34.

Den-ei shin seki The Filmmaker of the '90s Hou Hsiao-hsien (Tokyo: Pia, 1989).

Doane, Mary Ann. *The Dialogical Text: Filmic Irony and the Spectator* (Ann Arbor: University of Michigan Microfilms International, 1979).

Doane, Mary Ann, Patricia Mellencamp, and Linda Williams, eds. *Re-Vision: Essays in Feminist Film Criticism* (Frederick, MD: University Publications of America, 1984).

Dominic, Mart, and Peter Delpeut. "A Man Must Be Greater Than His Films." *Screen* (Holland) (January 1989). Reprinted in Japanese in *Den-ei shin seki The Filmmaker of the '90s Hou Hsiao-hsien,* 12–16 (Tokyo: Pia, 1989).

Du, Yunzhi. *Zhongguo dianying shi* [A history of Chinese cinema]. 3 vols. (Taipei: Shangwuyin, 1972).

Flant, Antony, and David Vasse, eds. *Le cinéma de Hou Hsiao-hsien: Escapes, temps, sons* (Rennes: Presses Universitaires de Rennes, 2013).

Frodon, Jean-Michel, ed. *Hou Hsiao-hsien* (Lonrai: Editions Cahiers du cinema, 1999).

Gabriel, Teshome. "Colonialism and 'Law and Order' Criticism." *Screen* 27.3–4 (1986): 140–47.

Gabriel, Teshome. *Third Cinema in the Third World: The Aesthetics of Liberation* (Ann Arbor: UMI Research Press, 1982).

Guest, Haden. "Reflections on the Screen: Hou Hsiao Hsien's *Dust in the Wind* and the Rhythms of the Taiwan New Cinema." In *Island on the Edge: Taiwan New Cinema and After,* ed. Chris Berry and Feii Lu, 27–38 (Hong Kong: Hong Kong University Press, 2005).

Haddon, Rosemary. "Hou Hsiao Hsien's *City of Sadness*: History and the Dialogic Female Voice." In *Island on the Edge: Taiwan New Cinema and After,* ed. Chris Berry and Feii Lu, 55–66 (Hong Kong: Hong Kong University Press, 2005).

Hasumi, Shigehiko. "Gamen o tsukuru no wa, kekkyoku, chokkan da to omou" [I Think Making a Scene Is, in the Final Instance, Intuition]. *Lumiere* (Tokyo) 9 (Fall 1989): 87–94.

Hasumi, Shigehiko. *Kantoku Ozu Yasujiro* [Director Ozu Yasujiro] (Tokyo: Chikuma Shobo, 1983).

Higson, Andrew. "The Concept of National Cinema." *Screen* 30.4 (1989): 36–47.

Hijojoshi [*City of Sadness*], *Chanter Cine* 2.14 (Tokyo: France Eigasha, 1990).

Hillenbrand, Margaret. "Trauma and the Politics of Identity: Form and Function in Fictional Narratives of the February 28th Incident." *Modern Chinese Literature and Culture* 17.2 (Fall 2005): 49–89.

Historical Research Commission of Taiwan. *The Historiographical Records on the Taiwan Event of February 28, 1947* (Tai-chung, Taiwan: Historical Research Commission Council of Taiwan Province, 1990).

Hobermann, J. "Hou Hsiao-hsien: The Edge of the World." *In Vulgar Modernism: Writing on Movies and Other Media,* 104–7 (Philadelphia: Temple University Press, 1991).

Huang, Edwin. "Cinema: Urban Anxieties." *Free China Review* 38.2 (February 1988): 30–32.

Hung, Christine Yu-ting. *A Nation of Sadness? A Study of History, Culture, and Gender in Hou Hsiao-hsien's Film* A City of Sadness (Germany: Lambert Academic Publishing, 2013).

Institute of Modern History. *Oral History 3: Special Issue on the February 28 Incident* (Taipei: Institute of Modern History, Academia Sinica, 1992).

Institute of Modern History. *The 228 Incident: A Documentary Collection.* Vol. 1 (Taipei: Institute of Modern History, Academia Sinica, 1992).

James, Caryn. "Postwar 'Sadness' in Taiwan." *New York Times* (6 October 1989): C13.

Johnson, Claire. *Notes on Women's Cinema* (London: Society for Education in Film and Television, 1975).

Kaldis, Nick. "Compulsory Orientalism: Hou Hsiao Hsien's *Flowers of Shanghai.*" In *Island on the Edge: Taiwan New Cinema and After,* ed. Chris Berry and Feii Lu, 127–36 (Hong Kong: Hong Kong University Press, 2005).

Kaplan, E. Ann. "Problematizing Cross-Cultural Analysis: The Case of Women in the Recent Chinese Cinema." *Wide Angle* 11.2 (1989): 40–50.

Kasman, Daniel. "Hou Hsiao-hsien's Urban Female Youth Trilogy." *Senses of Cinema* 39 (May 2006). http://sensesofcinema.com/2006/39/hou_urban_female_youth/.

Kauffmann, Stanley. "Elsewhere." *New Republic* 202.24 (11 June 1990): 26.

Kehr, David. "Director Makes Ordinary Life Extraordinary." *Chicago Tribune* (from Toronto Film Festival catalog, September 1989).

Kerr, George. *Formosa Betrayed* (New York: De Capo Press, 1976).

Kerr, George. *The Taiwan Confrontation Crisis* (Berkeley, CA: Formosan Association for Public Affairs, 1986).

Kinder, Marsha. "The Subversive Potential of the Pseudo-Iterative." *Film Quarterly* 43.2 (1989–90): 2–16.

Kristeva, Julia. *The Kristeva Reader*. Trans. Toril Moi (New York: Columbia University Press, 1986).

Lai Tse-han, Ramon H. Myers, and Wei Wou. *A Tragic Beginning: Taiwan Uprising of February 28, 1947* (Stanford: Stanford University Press, 1991).

Lamley, Harry, J. "Book review, *A Tragic Beginning: Taiwan Uprising of February 28, 1947.*" *Journal of Asian Studies* 51.3 (1992): 652–54.

Leyda, Jay. *Dianying: An Account of Films and the Film Audience in China* (Cambridge: MIT Press, 1972).

Li, Shangren. "Taiwan xindianying yu disandianying: yie changshiwing de bijiao" [The Taiwan New Cinema and Third Cinema: A tentative comparison] *Dianying xinshang* [Film Appreciation Journal] 5.2 (1987): 23–26.

Li, Tuo. "Narratives of History in the Cinematography of Hou Xiaoxian." *positions* 1.3 (Winter 1993): 805–15.

Li, Yongwei, and Xiaofen Peng. "Taiwan 'Xindianying' shiqi wei gongzouahe fangwenlu" [An interview with seventeen filmmakers in the Taiwan New Cinema movement] *Dianying xinshang* [Film Appreciation Journal] 5.2 (1987): 5–16.

Li, Youxin. "Gangtai liuda daoyian" [Six great directors from Hong Kong and Taiwan], *Zili Zaoba* [Independent Morning Post (Taipei)], 1986.

Liao, Ping-hui. "Lishi de yangqi?—zailun *Beiqing chengshi*" [Leaving history behind?—Rethinking *A City of Sadness*], *Zili Zaoba* [Independent Morning Post (Taipei)], (27 February 1991): 14.

Liao, Ping-hui. "Passing and Re-articulation of Identity: Memory, Trauma, and Cinema." *Tamkang Review* 29.4 (Summer 1999): 85–114.

Liao, Ping-hui. "Rewriting Taiwanese National History: The February 28 Incident as Spectacle." *Public Culture* 5 (1993): 281–96.

Lin, Sylvia Li-chun. "Screening Atrocity." In *Representing Atrocity in Taiwan: The 2/28 Incident and White Terror in Fiction and Film*, 128–53 (New York: Columbia University Press, 2007).

Lin, Wen-chi, Shiao-ying Shen and Jerome Li. *Xilian rensheng: Hou Hsiao-hsien dianying yanjiu* [Passionate detachment: Films of Hou Hsiao-hsien] (Taipei: Rye Field Publishing, 2000).

Liu, Senyiao. "Cong *Fenggui lai de ren* kan dianying de xieshi zhuyi" [*The Boys from Fenggui* and realism], *Shijie Dianying* [World Cinema Journal] 132 (1983): 50–54.

Lu, Fei-yi. *Taiwan dianying: Zhengzhi, jingji, meixue* [Taiwan cinema: Politics, economics and aesthetics] (Taipei: Yuanliu, 1998).

Lu, Sheldon H. and Emilie Yueh-yu Yeh. eds. *Chinese-Language Film: Historiography, Poetics, Politics* (Honolulu: University of Hawaii Press, 2005).

Lu, Tong-lin. "From a Voiceless Father to a Father's Voice: Hou Xiaoxian, *A Time* to Live and a Time to Die, A City of Sadness, The Puppetmaster.*" In *Confronting Modernity in the Cinemas of Taiwan and Mainland China,* 95–115 (Cambridge: Cambridge University Press, 2002).

Lupke, Christopher. "Chu T'ien-wen and the *Sotto Voce* of Gendered Expression in the Films of Hou Hsiao-hsien." In *Chinese Women's Cinema: Transnational Contexts,* ed. Lingzhen Wang, 274–92 (New York: Columbia University Press, 2011).

Lupke, Christopher. "The Muted Interstices of Testimony: *A City of Sadness* and the Predicament of Multiculturalism in Taiwan." *Asian Cinema* 15.1 (Spring 2004): 5–36.

Ma, Jean. "Time without Measure, Sadness without Cure." In *Melancholy Drift: Marking Time in Chinese Cinema,* 19–49 (Hong Kong: Hong Kong University Press, 2010).

Ma, Ning. "Symbolic Representation and Symbolic Violence: Chinese Family Melodrama of the Early 1980s." *East-West Film Journal* 4.1 (1989): 79–112.

Ma, Ning. "The Textual and Critical Difference of Being Radical: Reconstructing Chinese Leftist Films of the 1930s." *Wide Angle* 11.2 (1989): 22–31.

Marchetti, Gina. "The Blossoming of a Revolutionary Aesthetics: Xie Jin's *Two Stage Sisters.*" *Jump Cut* 34 (1989): 95–106.

Mendal, Douglas. *The Politics of Formosan Nationalism* (Berkeley: University of California Press, 1970).

Mi Zou, and Xinhua Liang, eds. *Xingdianying zhe ze* [The death of the New Cinema] (Taipei: Tangshang, 1991).

Modleski, Tania. "Time and Desire in the Woman's Film." *Cinema Journal* 23.3 (1984): 19–30.

Mulvey, Laura. "Visual Pleasure and Narrative Cinema." In *Visual and Other Pleasures,* 14–28 (Bloomington: Indiana University Press, 1989).

Ng, Yvonne. "Essence and Ellipsis in Hou Hsiao-hsien's *The Puppetmaster.*" *Kinema* (Spring 1999). http://www.kinema.uwaterloo.ca/article.php?id=213&feature.

Noh, David. "Taiwanese Director's *Sadness* Recalls Island's Turbulent Past." *Film Journal International* (New York) 93.2 (February 1990): 28.

Nornes, Abé Mark. "Hou Hsiao-hsien and Narrative Space." In *Hou Hsiao-hsien,* ed. Richard Suchenski, 154–68. (Vienna: Österreichisches Filmmuseum; and New York: Columbia University Press, 2014).

Nornes, Markus. "Terrorizer." *Film Quarterly* 8.2 (Spring 1989): 64–72.

Pines, Jim, and Paul Willemen. *Questions of Third Cinema* (London: British Film Institute, 1989).

Qi, Longren. "Cinema: Critiquing the Critics." *Free China Review* 38.2 (February 1988): 26–29.

Rawnsley, Ming-yeh. T. "Cinema, Historiography, and Identities in Taiwan: Hou Hsiao-hsien's *A City of Sadness.*" *Asian Cinema* 22.2 (2011): 196–213.

Rayns, Tony. *"Beiqing chengshi"* [*A City of Sadness*]. *Monthly Film Bulletin* 57 (June 1990): 152–54.

Rayns, Tony. "Hou Hsiao-hsien: Songs for Swinging Lovers." *Sight and Sound* 16.8 (August 2006): 14, 16–19.

Rayns, Tony. "The Position of Women in New Chinese Cinema." *East-West Film Journal* 1.2 (1987): 32–44.

Rayns, Tony. *"The Sandwich Man*: Between Taiwan and the Mainland, between the Real and the Surreal: Tony Rayns Talks to Hou Xiaoxian." *Monthly Film Bulletin* 55 (June 1988): 163–64.

Rayns, Tony. *"Tongnian Wangshi" [A Time to Live and a Time to Die].* *Monthly Film Bulletin* 55 (June 1988): 161–63.

Reynaud, Berenice. *A City of Sadness* (London: British Film Institute, 2002).

Rich, B. Ruby. "In the Name of Feminist Film Criticism." In *Jump Cut: Hollywood Politics and Counter Cinema,* ed. Peter Steven, 209–30 (New York: Praeger, 1985).

Richie, Donald. *Ozu* (Berkeley: University of California Press, 1974).

Said, Edward. *Orientalism* (New York: Vintage, 1981).

Salt, Barry. "Statistical Style Analysis of Motion Pictures." In *Movies and Methods,* vol. 2, 691–702 (Berkeley: University of California Press, 1985).

Scott, Jay. "A Cause for Rejoicing in a *City of Sadness." Globe and Mail* (Toronto) (15 September 1989).

Semsel, George. *Chinese Film: The State of the Art in the People's Republic of China* (New York: Praeger, 1987).

Semsel, George. *Chinese Film Theory: A Guide to the New Era* (New York: Praeger, 1990).

Shen, Shiao-ying. "Permutations of the Foreign/er: A Study of the Works of Edward Yang, Stan Lai, Chang Yi, and Hou Hsiao-Hsien." (PhD diss., National Central University Film Studies Center, 1995).

Silverman, Kaja. *The Acoustic Mirror* (Bloomington: Indiana University Press, 1988).

Sklar, Robert. "Hidden History, Modern Hedonism: The Films of Hou Hsiao-hsien." *Cineaste* 27.4 (Fall 2002): 11.

Stacey, Judith. *Patriarchy and Socialist Revolution in China* (Berkeley: University of California Press, 1983).

Stanbrook, Alan. "The Worlds of Hou Hsiao-hsien." *Sight and Sound* (1990): 120–24.

Stratton, David. *"Beiqing chengshi (A City of Sadness)." Variety* (20–26 September 1989): 30.

Tam, Kwok-kan, and Wimal Dissanayake. "Hou Hsiao-Hsien: Critical Encounters with Memory and History." In *New Chinese Cinema,* ed. Tam Kwok-kan and Wimal Dissanayake, 46–59 (Hong Kong: Oxford University Press, 1998).

Udden, James. "Hou Hsiao-hsien and the Question of a Chinese Style." *Asian Cinema* 13.2 (Fall–Winter 2002): 54–75.

Udden, James. *No Man an Island: The Cinema of Hou Hsiao-hsien* (Hong Kong: Hong Kong University Press, 2009).

Udden, James. "Taiwanese Popular Cinema and the Strange Apprenticeship of Hou Hsiao-hsien." *Modern Chinese Literature and Culture* 15.1 (Spring 2003): 120–45.

Udden, James. "'This Time He Moves!' The Deeper Significance of Hou Hsiao-hsien's Radical Break in *Good Men, Good Women.*" In *Cinema Taiwan: Politics, Popularity and State of the Arts,* ed. Darrell William Davis and Ru-shou Robert Chen, 183–202 (London: Routledge, 2007).

"Victory in Venice Is a Tribute to Taiwanese Effort." *Variety* (27 September–3 October 1989): 30.

Wan, Xuting. "Liti de dianying—*Beiqing chengshi* de kongjian yu xushi" [A film that fails to cover its subject—the space and narrative of *City of Sadness*], *Zili Zaobau* [Independent Morning Post (Taipei)], (8 December 1989): 14.

Warner, Charles R. "Smoke Gets in Your Eyes: Hou Hsiao-hsien's Optics of Ephemerality." *Senses of Cinema* 39 (May 2006). http://sensesofcinema.com/2006/39/hou_optics_ephemerality/.

Wu, I-fen. "Looking for Nostalgia: Memory and National Identity in *A Time to Live, a Time to Die*." *Cineaction* 60.1 (2003): 45–51.

Wu, Qiyan. "Lishijiyi, dianying yishu yu zhengzhi" [Historical memory, cinematic arts, and politics], *Dianying xinshang* [Film Appreciation Journal] 8.3 (1991): 41–43.

Wu, Qiyan. "Taiwan jingyan de yingxiang suzao" [Construction of the image of Taiwan's experience], *Dianying xinshang* [Film Appreciation Journal] 8.2 (1991): 50–52.

Wu, Zhenghuan. "Hou Hsiao-hsien dianying de liangge shijie" [The two worlds of Hou Hsiao-hsien's film], *Dianying xinshang* [Film Appreciation Journal] 5.2 (1987): 6–21.

Yan, Huizeng. "Shiyi xieshi zhuyi—Taiwan xindiangying yu yian chugao" [Poetic realism: A first draft of a discussion of the Taiwan New Cinema], *Dianying xinshang* [Film Appreciation Journal] 5.2 (1987): 17–22.

Yau, Esther. "Cultural and Economic Dislocations: Filmic Phantasies of Chinese Women in the 1980s." *Wide Angle* 11.2 (1989): 6–21.

Yau, Esther. "Is China the End of Hermeneutics? Or, Political and Cultural Usage of Non-Han Women in Mainland Chinese Film." *Discourse* 11.2 (1989): 115–36.

Yau, Esther. "*Yellow Earth*: A Western Analysis and a Non-Western Text." *Film Quarterly* 16.2 (1987–88): 22–33.

Yeh, Emilie Yueh-yu. "The Disappearing Act: Taiwan Popular Cinema." In *Contemporary Asian Cinema: Popular Culture in a Global Frame,* ed. Anne Ciecko, 156–68 (London: Berg Publications, 2006).

Yeh, Emilie Yueh-yu. "Poetics and Politics of Hou Hsiao-hsien's Films." In *Chinese-Language Film: Historiography, Poetics, Politics,* ed. Sheldon Lu and Emilie Yueh-yu Yeh, 163–85 (Honolulu: University of Hawai'i Press, 2005).

Yeh, Emilie Yueh-yu, and Darrell William Davis. *Taiwan Film Directors: A Treasure Island* (New York: Columbia University Press, 2005).

Yeh, Yueh-yu. "Nüren zhende wufa jinru lishi ma? Zai du *Beiqing chengshi*" [Why can't women enter history? Re-reviewing *City of Sadness*], *Dangdai* [Contemporary Monthly] 101 (September 1994): 64–85.

Yip, June. *Envisioning Taiwan: Fiction, Cinema, and the Nation in the Cultural Imaginary* (Durham, NC: Duke University Press, 2004).

Yoshimoto, Mitsuhiro. "The Postmodern and Mass Images of Japan." *Public Culture* 1.2 (1989): 8–25.

Yun, Eugenia. "Cinema: A Delicate Balance." *Free China Review* 38.2 (February 1988): 4–11.

Zhang, Longxi. "The Myth of the Other: China in the Eyes of the West." *Critical Inquiry* 15.1 (1988): 110–35.

Index

www.ingramcontent.com/pod-product-compliance
Lightning Source LLC
Chambersburg PA
CBHW070351270326
41926CB00017B/4088